Marilyn Hickey reminds us that it is impossible to [illegible]se God without faith. Who better to teach us than one of America's most beloved Bible teachers? Thank you, Marilyn…as always, you are clear and insightful.

Marcus & Joni Lamb
Daystar Television Network

Marilyn Hickey continues to mesmerize audiences and inspire readers with her innovative, insightful revelations from the Word of God. Every believer should read her thoughts!

Bishop T. D. Jakes, Sr.
The Potter's House of Dallas, Inc.

Marilyn Hickey is a powerful woman of faith. She speaks not only from theoretical knowledge, but also from experience wrought through the crucible of life. Through the Word of God as well as testimonies, quotes, and examples, Marilyn brings "faith" into the natural realm of everyday life. Journey with her as she encourages you to view life's experiences through eyes of faith.

Joyce Meyer
Best-selling author and Bible teacher

Marilyn Hickey has been a dear friend to Lisa and me for years. In her usual style that is both easy to understand and full of Scripture, Marilyn encourages us to explore what God has to say about faith. She expertly describes the difference between faith and hope and how the two work together to bring forth the promises of God. I recommend this book to all who want to grow in their walk with the Lord.

John Bevere

Dr. Marilyn Hickey is one of the world's foremost experts in the area of faith. I highly recommend her book on the subject of faith. All of God's glorious promises are activated by faith, and Dr. Hickey has provided a way to access this exciting and world-changing power.

Dr. David Yonggi Cho
CGI Chairman

WOW Faith

Bringing the Childlike Heart Back to Faith

WOW Faith

Bringing the Childlike Heart Back to Faith

Marilyn Hickey

WOW FAITH

Marilyn Hickey Ministries
PO Box 17340
Denver, CO 80217

ISBN 1-880809-99-0
Printed in the United States of America

Previously published as *Mega Faith*, ISBN 1-56441-045-5, by Marilyn Hickey Ministries.

Legacy Publishers International
1301 South Clinton Street
Denver, CO 80247
www.legacypublishersinternational.com

Cover design by: Kirk DouPonce, UDGdesignworks

2 3 4 5 6 7 8 9 10 11 / 09 08 07 06 05 04

TABLE OF CONTENTS

PREFACE

Dear Friend,

Often, when we are experiencing hard times, people encourage us to "just have faith." That's good advice—as long as we understand what faith really is. Some think that having faith means sitting back and doing nothing, but true faith is alive and active.

Developing an active faith—a faith that gets results—is a journey, and this book is a guide to lead you on that path. I am thrilled that you have chosen to walk this road with me to a more dynamic and rewarding faith, and I know you will be greatly blessed with each step you take.

God has given us the *"measure of faith"* to sustain us: *"Now faith is the assurance of things hoped for, the conviction of things not seen"* (Hebrews 11:1). To have faith in God, we must believe in and believe for things we cannot see. This can be very difficult when we are surrounded and even overwhelmed by the visible world pressing in from all sides, demanding our attention.

The enemy would have us believe only in the troubles of this world, but true faith is living successfully in the visible world by trusting in the goodness of a God we cannot see. This world can weaken, even defeat us; faith gives us vitality and victory.

Throughout the chapters of this book, you will find stories of real people whose faith carried them through seemingly impossible circumstances. Your faith can do the same for you!

Here you will find the secrets to building a strong and active faith. You will learn the definition, fundamentals, and sources of an enduring faith. You also will learn how to guard against the greatest destroyers of faith, including your own tongue. Discover how faith can overcome your trials and help you get answers to your prayers. See faith in action in the lives of some well-known (and not-so-well-known) heroes and heroines in the Bible.

Most important of all, you will learn that true faith—strong, active faith that pleases God and gets results—is *simple* faith, *childlike* faith. Children are very trusting by nature, and they will believe what they are told unless people or experience teaches them otherwise. God wants us to approach Him with faith like that of a child: simple, trusting, persevering, and confident. That is the kind of faith that gets results and leads to health and victory.

This book springs from my prayer for you to experience the joy of living out a vigorous faith in all aspects of your life. I believe that as you read and practice the action plans at the end of each chapter, your faith will grow and grow, and you will be rewarded with confidence and prosperity. Burdens will be lighter, fears will evaporate, and your every need will be met.

In His love and mine,
Marilyn

CHAPTER ONE

Discover Faith—The Unseen Realm

One of the endearing qualities of children is their simple trust. To a point, children believe anything they are told, particularly by people older than themselves. That is why we must always be careful what we say to children; they will take us literally.

In 1904, the play *Peter Pan* premiered in London. At one point in the story, Peter told the Darling children that if they believed strongly enough that they could fly, they *would* fly. Soon after the play opened, Sir James Barrie, the author, began hearing from parents whose children had taken Peter's words literally, tried to fly, and injured themselves in the process. Barrie immediately added to the story a cautionary statement that children could fly *only* after first being sprinkled with "fairy dust." Since fairy dust was in short supply, there were no further incidents.[1]

Children take a very simple approach to faith: They simply *believe*. Trust is part of their nature, a reflection of the divine image of God in them. If parents or other grown-ups tell them about Santa Claus or the Easter Bunny, they assume it must be true. If someone says to them, "God loves you," they accept it without question.

As adults, we all see the world differently than we did when we were children. Do you remember the sense of wonder and joy of life you felt as a child? Everything was fresh and new and each day was an exciting new adventure waiting to be discovered. Life was full of smiles and laughter and games and friends and everything was right with the world.

Or was it? Perhaps your childhood was different. Perhaps you lived in a situation where you had to grow up quickly. Realities of life in your circumstances may have robbed you of a carefree childhood. Your memories of those years may be quite painful.

"The faith that pleases God is *child-like* faith."

Regardless of our individual experiences, something happens to our childlike view of life as we grow older. Part of maturity is learning how, in Paul's words, to *"put away childish things"* (1 Corinthians 13:11 NKJV). This means setting aside childish thoughts, ideas, attitudes, words, and behavior in favor of those of mature adults. Oftentimes, however, we also lose our simple, childlike approach to life somewhere along the way. Being *childish* and being *childlike* are not necessarily the same. Childishness has to do with immaturity, while childlikeness has to do with how we relate (or should relate) to God.

We relate to God through faith. Hebrews 11:6 says, *"Without faith it is impossible to please Him, for he who comes to God must believe that He is and that He is a rewarder of those who seek Him."* The kind of faith that pleases God is *childlike* faith—the simple, unquestioning trust like that of a child's. Jesus said, *"Truly I say to you, whoever does not receive the kingdom of God like a child will not enter it at all"* (Mark 10:15).

As we get older, life becomes very complicated. Our society has made it that way. We live in a fast-paced and high-pressure world—a complex society that seeks complex answers to every question. If an answer appears simple, it must be wrong. As a consequence, we have allowed even our faith to become complicated. Gone is the simple, childlike trust, and in its place is a confusing system of rules and conditions that offers more questions than answers.

For many Christians today, faith is a weighty burden rather than a source of joy and freedom. Saddled with heavy requirements laid on them by their particular church or group, these believers engage in a daily struggle to "prove" their faith or demonstrate that they have "enough" faith. How much faith is "enough"? Who determines that? How does a person make faith "work" in his or her life?

Perhaps you are one of those people. Do you often struggle with your faith even though you have been born again? Do you try to have strong faith, yet wonder why nothing seems to change in your life? Do you long to be close to God, yet find that your faith seems smaller than ever? Does it seem that no matter how hard you try, you simply can't get your faith to "work" for you? Do you wish you could return to the simple, childlike faith you once had?

You can!

God deliberately designed faith to be simple enough for a child to understand. We complicate it by adding "extras" and "options" that God never intended. In order to return to a childlike approach to faith, we must first distinguish between what the world calls faith, and faith as God has revealed it in His Word.

Faith: By Reason or by Revelation?

Faith means different things to different people and varies with the circumstance. Buddhists, Muslims, and Christians view faith differently from each other. An aircraft designer has "faith" in the laws of aerodynamics. A sports fan has "faith" in his favorite team. So what constitutes *God-pleasing* faith? Before we can answer that question, we must be clear about what we mean by the word *faith*. Let's begin with a basic definition. According to Webster's dictionary, faith is:

- allegiance to duty or to a person: loyalty
- fidelity to one's promises
- belief and trust in and loyalty to God
- firm belief in something for which there is no proof
- a system of religious beliefs.[2]

Certainly, biblical or God-pleasing faith involves the first three of these definitions: belief in and loyalty to God and fidelity or faithfulness in keeping our promises to Him (also known as obedience). Contrary to what many in the world would claim, faith in God is *not* a belief in something that has no proof. Evidence of the reality of God is all around us, plain to see for anyone who is willing to look. And finally, faith in the God of the Bible is far more than just a system of religious beliefs.

Every day we encounter different kinds or levels of faith. At one time or another we all have walked in these areas of worldly faith. Let's look at them briefly.

Human Faith

Human faith is the kind that even unbelievers talk about: faith that their business will succeed, faith in their mates or their family, faith in their career efforts, faith in their doctors, faith in the laws and discoveries of science. Human faith works in natural ways by natural processes. It is a belief in human achievement by human efforts and, in its place, is a legitimate form of belief.

Religious Faith

People with religious faith place their trust in a belief system such as Buddhism, Islam, or Hinduism, or in a particular creed, organization, church, or other religious body. On the surface, they may look and sound good and practice their religion diligently. Dig a little deeper, however, and it becomes clear that their faith revolves around what they *do*—outward observance of man-made ordinances, rituals, or traditions.

Experiential Faith

Experiential faith depends on visible proof. By his own admission, the faith of the apostle Thomas was based on what he could see and touch:

> *So the other disciples were saying to him, "We have seen the Lord!" But he said to them, "Unless I see in His hands the imprint of the nails, and put my finger into the place of the nails, and put my hand into His side, I will not believe"* (John 20:25).

Many people today are just like Thomas, believing only that which they can prove with their senses or reason with their minds. If they cannot experience it in tangible, personal form, they will not believe.

Intellectual Faith

Intellectual faith is giving mental assent to the principles of faith without putting the heart into it. Such "faith" will not cause anything to change in our lives. It is a mental belief that makes no moral demands. James was referring to intellectual faith when he wrote, *"Faith without works is dead"* (James 2:26). The rich young ruler believed the right things and lived a good life. He wanted eternal life but was not willing to involve his heart, make Jesus the Lord of his life, and follow and obey Him (see Luke 18:18–25). In the end, he went away *"very sad"* because he was unwilling to meet Jesus' demand. His intellectual faith was not enough.

Temporary Faith

Some people "get religion" during a crisis or trauma in their lives or in the hope of simply improving their own situation. Because they are never truly grounded in the basics of their belief, their faith soon slips away. In His parable of the sower and the seed, Jesus described these people as *"rocky places"*:

> *The one on whom seed was sown on the rocky places, this is the man who hears the word and immediately receives it with joy; yet he has no firm root in himself, but is only temporary, and when affliction or persecution arises because of the word, immediately he falls away* (Matthew 13:20–21).

Revelation Faith

This kind of faith is the result of God's Word being illuminated in our hearts by the Holy Spirit. It is a gift from Him:

> *For by grace you have been saved through faith; and that not of yourselves, it is the gift of God; not as a result of works, so that no one may boast* (Ephesians 2:8–9).

With revelation faith we can believe and act on our belief without confirmation or proof. Once the apostle Thomas had a chance to see the risen Christ for himself, his experiential faith changed to revelation faith. He no longer needed tangible evidence in order to believe. Revelation faith affects the visible world, but it comes from the *invisible* world—the realm of the kingdom of God. As its name indicates, it is a *revealed* faith. We cannot know this kind of faith by human senses or human reason alone; God must reveal it.

Jesus spoke of revelation faith in His parable of the sower and the seed when He said:

> *The one on whom seed was sown on the good soil, this is the man who hears the word and understands it; who indeed bears fruit and brings forth, some a hundredfold, some sixty, and some thirty* (Matthew 13:23).

Revelation faith is powerful; it commands any situation. We see this kind of faith in Jesus when He commanded winds to obey, diseases to flee, and the dead to be raised. When we have revelation faith, we expect the miracle-working power of God to operate, and therefore we are not surprised when miracles actually occur. True revelation faith is childlike faith. Just as a child implicitly trusts the words of his or her parents, so also do we trust the Word of God. Whatever God says, we simply believe.

Faith and Hope

Simple faith does not mean we reject our human intellect and reason, but it does mean we recognize that there are realities beyond those we can perceive with our five natural senses. In order to fully understand faith, we must realize that the world we cannot see (the invisible) is as real as the world we can see (the visible). We cannot see oxygen, but we breathe it for life—it is vital to our existence. How silly it would be to say that oxygen does not exist simply because we cannot see it! The invisible spiritual realm has just as much form and substance as the visible physical realm. Our faith enables us to "see" that invisible realm with spiritual eyes. The apostle Paul said, *"For we walk by faith, not by sight"* (2 Corinthians 5:7). In other words, we live not only according to what we can see, hear, taste, smell, and touch, but also by realities that God reveals to us that are beyond normal human perception.

"What we don't see is as real as what we do see."

When God reveals a truth from His Word, we do not always see immediate physical manifestation of it. This does not mean His Word is false; it only means that we cannot see the truth with our eyes or perceive it with our senses. Placing our trust in God means believing in that which we cannot touch or see:

> *We look not at the things which are seen, but at the things which are not seen; for the things which are seen are temporal, but the things which are not seen are eternal* (2 Corinthians 4:18).

Faith is vital to life; without it, we *cannot* please God. Maybe you desire with all your heart to please God and be like Him, yet feel that you simply cannot squeeze out another ounce of faith. Who says you have to? So often we complicate faith by making it too hard. Besides, we are not even capable of producing God-pleasing faith in our own strength, so why try? In order to please God and be like Him, we must have *His* kind of faith, which He alone can give.

It is a matter of simple trust: God-pleasing faith believes that God is and that He rewards those who seek Him (see Hebrews 11:6). Even children understand trust, and they understand rewards as well. When people seek God, He rewards them with faith. That is why God-pleasing faith is available to *anyone*. Our faith depends not on our level of education, how much money we make, or how holy we appear to be to others, but on our willingness to abandon everything to God and simply trust Him alone.

Faith is a lifestyle, not a formula. Habakkuk 2:4 says, *"The righteous will live by his faith."* Paul expanded on this thought when he wrote to the Romans:

> *For I am not ashamed of the gospel, for it is the power of God for salvation to everyone who believes, to the Jew first and also to the Greek. For in it the righteousness of God is revealed from faith to faith; as it is written, "But the righteous man shall live by faith"* (Romans 1:16–17).

The key to righteousness—right standing with God—is to live by faith in the Person of Jesus Christ as the Son of God and as Savior and Lord of all. This is the faith that pleases God. Jesus said, *"This is the work of God, that you believe in Him whom He has sent"* (John 6:29). Does this describe *your* faith? Are you trusting simply in the Lord alone, or has your faith become complicated by a lot of "add-ons"? If so, what do you do? The Word of God will help you understand His kind of faith and how to attain it.

So then, what exactly *is* faith? What does it mean to *believe*? The classic biblical definition of faith is found in the eleventh chapter of Hebrews:

> *Now faith is the assurance of things hoped for, the conviction of things not seen* (Hebrews 11:1).

The King James Version is slightly different:

Now faith is the substance of things hoped for, the evidence of things not seen (Hebrews 11:1).

This verse identifies two major components of faith: first, the *assurance* or *substance* or confirmation of the things we hoped for, and second, the *conviction* or *evidence* or proof of what we cannot see. In other words, faith means being absolutely convinced of the truth of God's promises even in the absence of physical evidence. It means being so convinced that we live and act as if the things we hope for are already ours.

"Faith is a lifestyle, not a formula."

Hope is more than wishful thinking—it is the vision in faith of our desire. Although it is true that hope alone cannot make something happen, hope and faith together, intertwined as partners, are very powerful. One good definition of hope is "to anticipate, usually with pleasure and confidence." Biblical hope is grounded in the certainty of God's Word and is a confident expectation of receiving everything that He has promised. Faith feeds hope and inspires us to take the actions necessary to help bring to pass the things we hope for.

What are you hoping for today? What needs in your life call for an active and effective faith? Maybe you have a financial need. Perhaps you need healing or desire resolution of a difficult circumstance. Whatever your need, here are a couple of tips to help you cultivate your faith:

1. Keep your hope—your desire—clearly in front of you.
2. Exercise your faith continuously by acting as though God's Word is true and real, even though you cannot yet see the results. Say, "Although I can't see it yet, I know I have it because I know God's Word is true and He cannot lie."

Like faith, hope is vital to life. We cannot cope without hope! It is a known fact that people battling serious illness are much more likely to die if they lose hope of recovery. Once they lose hope, they lose the will to live, and when they lose the will to live, they usually decline very rapidly. Faith gives substance to our hope. If we hope in the Lord, we can be confident that our hope will not be disappointed:

> *Therefore, having been justified by faith, we have peace with God through our Lord Jesus Christ, through whom also we have obtained our introduction by faith into this grace in which we stand; and we exult in hope of the glory of God...and hope does not disappoint, because the love of God has been poured out within our hearts through the Holy Spirit who was given to us* (Romans 5:1–2, 5).

As long as we have hope, we can cope with any situation, circumstance, or adversity that comes along, as well as anything the devil sends our way.

Sometimes we have to keep hoping even when it looks like all hope is gone. Abraham and Sarah, already well beyond normal child-bearing age, waited twenty-five years for the birth of their son Isaac as God had promised. They never lost hope despite the fact that they were too old to have children. God fulfilled His promise. Abraham was one hundred years old and Sarah ninety when Isaac was born. *"In hope against hope he believed, so that he might become a father of many nations, according to that which had been spoken, 'So shall your descendants be' "* (Romans 4:18). If Abraham's faith had been based solely upon his circumstances, his hope probably would have been shattered. However, Abraham's hope was in God—and he received his promise!

"We cannot cope without hope!"

You may be thinking, *That's all fine and good, but hope is either there or it isn't. I can't just manufacture it.* That is true. *We* cannot create hope, but God's Word can! Feed on it daily and it will develop hope in your spirit:

> *Remember the word to Your servant, in which You have made me hope* (Psalm 119:49).

> *Sustain me according to Your word, that I may live; and do not let me be ashamed of my hope* (Psalm 119:116).

> *I wait for the Lord, my soul does wait, and in His word do I hope* (Psalm 130:5).

> *Because of the hope laid up for you in heaven, of which you previously heard in the word of truth, the gospel* (Colossians 1:5).

The more Word you receive into your spirit, the more your hope will grow, and the stronger your faith will become.

Hatching Your Faith

In his book *The Fourth Dimension*, Dr. David Yonggi Cho says that faith goes through an incubation period before the answer can be seen or felt. The word *incubation* describes a time of patient waiting, such as "sitting on (eggs) to hatch" or "causing something to develop (such as an idea)." Do you want to "hatch" a stronger and more effective faith? Consider the following steps:

First, visualize a clear-cut picture of the objective of your faith. As you *meditate* on God's Word, *visualize* your objective coming to pass. For example, if you are meditating on healing, visualize your body well. Get a clear-cut picture in mind—and be specific!

Dr. Cho recounts that during his early ministry, he was without a desk, a chair, and a bicycle—so he asked the Lord for them. He expected these items to arrive at any time. One month passed, then two. Nothing. Three months went by and still nothing happened. After six months had passed with no answer, Dr. Cho became discouraged. He felt he had a responsibility to be an example of faith for those around him, yet could not seem to get such a simple request as this answered.

One day he cried out, "What's wrong, Lord?" God answered and told him to be more specific in his requests. His answer had not come because he had not expressed a clear-cut vision. Immediately, he spelled out his request to the Lord. "Please, Lord, send me a Philippine mahogany desk (of a certain size), an iron-frame chair with rollers, and an American-made bicycle." The Lord brought a Scripture to his mind to help him maintain his faith until he received his answer: *"God...calleth those things which be not as though they were"* (Romans 4:17 KJV).

Dr. Cho explained to his congregation that just as a baby is in its mother's womb nine months before its birth, so he had "conceived" a desk, a chair, and a bicycle. Soon after, he received exactly what he had requested.

Second, you must have a burning desire for the thing you request. God rewards the earnest seeker, not the casual inquirer. You can't be laid-back and nonchalant in your requests and expect to get answers. So make sure that what you request is something you really need and want and something that is consistent with God's will and purpose. Red-hot desire gets results: *"Delight yourself in the LORD; and He will give you the desires of your heart"* (Psalm 37:4).

Third, pray for assurance of the answer. Since faith is the *"assurance of things hoped for,"* you need to put in your heart the assurance of the answer. Your assurance, or guarantee, is like the title deed to "the thing hoped for." Now that you have made your request, *trust* the Lord to answer in His time and in His way. Consider your answer as certain as if you already had it in hand.

Finally, speak the Word into your situation. Speak the Word during the "incubation period"—and speak it boldly! That is the process: *visualize, desire, pray,* and *speak*. While waiting for the answer, you may need to repeat the cycle, perhaps many times, to keep exercising and nurturing your faith.

When Joshua and Caleb returned from spying out the land of Canaan, they spoke boldly about what they believed. Although they were in the minority, they did not allow themselves to be influenced by others. They boldly declared their faith.

Faith in your heart is not enough—you must release faith with your mouth: " *'The word is near you, in your mouth and in your heart'—that is, the word of faith*" (Romans 10:8).

Build on a Solid Foundation

Having faith doesn't mean much if it is focused in the wrong direction. The only way to have an effective faith—a faith that gets results—is to build it on a solid foundation. God, your heavenly Father, created you to live in fellowship with Him in faith. He has wonderful plans for you, His chosen creation, and He wants you to grow in maturity and wisdom. When you walk in a love relationship with God, He causes all things to work together for your good! This does not mean that things will run smoothly in your life all the time, but it does mean that God will use even your battles to strengthen and bless you. Bad things *do* happen because the world is dominated by sin and Satan, but God takes care of His own. Paul stated it this way:

> *And we know that God causes all things to work together for good to those who love God, to those who are called according to His purpose* (Romans 8:28).

You may be asking, "How can I *know* that God is trustworthy as the foundation for my faith? How can I be sure that He loves me and will always take care of me?" Simply look at what the Bible reveals about Him:

God is supreme. This means that He is the best of the best, the greatest of all, the utmost, higher than the highest, deeper than the deepest—absolutely unequalled in all the universe! God is *omnipotent* (all-powerful), *omniscient* (all-knowing), and *omnipresent* (present everywhere). He has the power to meet even the greatest need in your life. He knows everything about you and is aware of everything that happens to you. Ever present everywhere, He is always close to you. There is nowhere you can go and be away from God's loving presence. The psalmist wrote, *"Where can I go from Your Spirit? Or where can I flee from Your presence? If I ascend to heaven, You are there; if I make my bed in Sheol, behold, You are there"* (Psalm 139:7–8).

God is just. He is fair and equitable in all His dealings. To say that God is just means that He does only what is right. Rest assured that God will always treat you fairly. He can never be accused of evil, partiality, or unfairness.

God is true. You can trust God to mean what He says and to carry out what He promises. He keeps His Word and His Word will accomplish all that He sends it forth to do: *"So will My word be which goes forth from My mouth; it will not return to Me empty, without accomplishing what I desire, and without succeeding in the matter for which I sent it"* (Isaiah 55:11).

God is faithful. God Himself operates by faith, and as His child you should imitate Him: *"Therefore be imitators of God, as beloved children"* (Ephesians 5:1). He desires for you to be full of faith because His very character is faithfulness: *"If we are faithless, He remains faithful, for He cannot deny Himself"* (2 Timothy 2:13).

How faithful is God? Consider these Scriptures:

> *Forever, O Lord, Your word is settled in heaven. Your faithfulness continues throughout all generations; You established the earth, and it stands* (Psalm 119:89–90).

> *The* Lord*'s lovingkindnesses indeed never cease, for His compassions never fail. They are new every morning; great is Your faithfulness.* (Lamentations 3:22–23).

> *God is faithful, through whom you were called into fellowship with His Son, Jesus Christ our Lord* (1 Corinthians 1:9).

> *Faithful is He who calls you, and He also will bring it to pass* (1 Thessalonians 5:24).

These are only a few of the attributes of God that demonstrate that He is absolutely worthy of your complete trust.

As the living Word of God, Jesus is one with the Father: *"Do not let your heart be troubled; you believe in God, believe also in Me. ...He who has seen Me has seen the Father....Believe Me that I am in the Father and the Father is in Me"* (John 14:1, 9b, 11a). The writer of Hebrews calls Jesus *"the author and finisher of our faith"* (Hebrews 12:2b NKJV). Jesus is the rock, the solid foundation on which our faith is built. He said as much at the end of His Sermon on the Mount:

> *Therefore everyone who hears these words of Mine and acts on them, may be compared to a wise man who built his house on the rock. And the rain fell, and the floods came, and the winds blew and slammed against that house; and yet it did not fall, for it had been founded on the rock* (Matthew 7:24–25).

Can God be trusted? Absolutely! Place your faith confidently in the one who loves you and will never fail you. The basis for your faith is the Word of a God who has shown Himself to be totally reliable. Childlike faith is not "blind" faith, but faith that is based on the revealed truth of God. Just as a child implicitly trusts his parents, you too can trust completely your heavenly Father, who is righteous, faithful, and trustworthy.

A Covenant for Your Family

One exciting aspect of God's faithfulness is that when we walk in the truth of His Word, He will watch over our children and our children's children! This is His promise:

Know therefore that the LORD your God, He is God, the faithful God, who keeps His covenant and His lovingkindness to a thousandth generation with those who love Him and keep His commandments (Deuteronomy 7:9).

My family is my first priority and when I travel I think of them often. It is easy for me to start worrying about them: "How are they doing? Are they all right?" Whenever that happens, I try to remember to bring my mind back into line: "Wait a minute! Early this morning I spoke God's Word into every situation at home and I rest in that." The Lord gives an incredible peace when we entrust everything into His loving and capable hands.

Rest assured that God keeps His promises! He will never let you down! His Word will work in any situation that you can possibly imagine. Nothing in the world is more powerful than the Word of God. If God can hold up the world with a single word, He can certainly take care of you and your loved ones, as well as mine.

I experienced this truth in a dramatic way when our daughter Sarah was in kindergarten. The church had arranged a special luncheon for ladies and great care had been taken to plan the event well. As the pastor's wife, I had a responsibility to be there, even though normally I picked Sarah up at the bus stop at that time. That day, I asked a woman from our church to meet Sarah for me. I gave the woman specific and detailed directions about where Sarah would get off the bus.

After repeating the instructions to make sure they were clear, I put my mind at rest so I could concentrate on the luncheon. Eighteen hundred people attended and many souls were saved. Some ladies even got saved out in the parking lot! It was a wonderful, victorious day!

In the meantime, five-year-old Sarah had an adventure of her own! She got off her bus, looked around for someone to meet her, then sat down on the grass and waited—and waited—and *waited*. The woman who was to meet her had gotten the directions confused and was waiting two blocks away. After an hour this lady panicked and returned to the church.

Sarah remembered to pray: "God, I need to get home, so You show me how to go. Thank You, God."

Oh, the wonderful simplicity of a child's faith! Near our house was a canal that Sarah had to cross to get home. She did not want to get her shoes muddy, so she prayed again, "Dear God, please show me how to cross the canal so I won't get my feet wet and muddy." She told us later how the Lord led her to a place where there were rocks so she could cross the canal safely "on dry land."

Her next hurdle was getting inside the house. We had put an emergency key in a safe place that she could reach. She found it, but had never before unlocked the door by herself. Nevertheless, she managed to let herself in the house, where she called the church office and reached my administrative assistant.

"Sarah, where are you? Are you all right?" When Sarah told her she was at home, my administrative assistant went quickly and picked her up, so all ended well.

It wasn't over for me yet, however. "God, this is terrible, absolutely terrible! I'm never going to do this kind of thing again. I can't be running around trying to have a big event when my children need me. Never again!"

Then I heard the Lord speak into my spirit. "Isn't Sarah all right?" He asked.

"Yes, Lord, she is."

"Did I take care of her?"

"Yes, Lord, You did."

Suddenly, I knew where He was going with this. "When you are about My business, I am about your business." Now, this does not mean that I can neglect my family and expect Him to intervene, but it does mean that God is faithful when we are faithful. Don't be afraid to trust God. Commit yourself to His business and He will take care of yours. You can count on it!

A Lifetime Guarantee!

Do you need a faith boost? Your heavenly Father has filled His Word with promises that apply to you and your loved ones and that carry a lifetime guarantee! As long as you are walking by faith and seeking to honor the Lord, you can claim His promises as yours. How can you know God's promises are valid? He has *guaranteed* them by swearing upon His own integrity:

For when God made the promise to Abraham, since He could swear by no one greater, He swore by Himself (Hebrews 6:13).

An excellent medicine for strengthening your faith would be to search the Scriptures for every promise of God you can find. The more you know what God has said, the more your faith will grow, and the more confident you will be in turning the affairs of your life over to Him in simple, childlike trust. Here are some truths and promises from God's Word to help you get started.

1. God's Word is full of promises to touch every part of your life:

   Forever, O Lord, Your word is settled in heaven (Psalm 119:89).

2. His Word endures, and it will never pass away:

   The grass withers, the flower fades, but the word of our God stands forever (Isaiah 40:8).

   "As for Me, this is My covenant with them," says the Lord: "My Spirit which is upon you, and My words which I have put in your mouth shall not depart from your mouth, nor from the mouth of your offspring, nor from the mouth of your offspring's offspring," says the Lord, "from now and forever" (Isaiah 59:21).

3. God pledges His Word is valid and true:

   As for God, His way is blameless; the word of the Lord is tested; He is a shield to all who take refuge in Him (2 Samuel 22:31).

4. God's Word is refined and pure as gold. When you read the Word, you never have to wonder if it has been watered down:

   The words of the Lord are pure words; as silver tried in a furnace on the earth, refined seven times (Psalm 12:6).

5. God's Word is righteous:

   For the word of the Lord is upright, and all His work is done in faithfulness (Psalm 33:4).

6. The Word is truth and the promises of God were confirmed in Christ Jesus:

   Sanctify them in the truth; Your word is truth (John 17:17).

7. Jesus went about healing all who were sick, so we know that God's Word has healing power:

   He sent His word and healed them, and delivered them from their destructions (Psalm 107:20).

8. Whatever struggle you are in, whether it be grief, stress, or financial or physical problems, the promises of the Word are your strength:

   My soul weeps because of grief; strengthen me according to Your word (Psalm 119:28).

9. When you need light or understanding, wisdom or guidance, turn to God's Word:

   The unfolding of Your words gives light; it gives understanding to the simple (Psalm 119:130).

10. His Word endures:

    Heaven and earth will pass away, but My words shall not pass away (Matthew 24:35).

11. His Word is valid:

    Every word of God is tested; He is a shield to those who take refuge in Him (Proverbs 30:5).

12. His Word is powerful:

    For with God nothing is ever impossible and no word from God shall be without power or impossible of fulfillment (Luke 1:37 AMP).

13. His Word is for you now:

> *My son, observe the commandment of your father and do not forsake the teaching of your mother; bind them continually on your heart; tie them around your neck. When you walk about, they will guide you; when you sleep, they will watch over you; and when you awake, they will talk to you. For the commandment is a lamp and the teaching is light; and reproofs for discipline are the way of life* (Proverbs 6:20–23).

14. God's Word brings salvation and then becomes your textbook for life. That is why it is vitally important to know the Word—its promises—and to understand that they belong to you *now*:

> *But these have been written so that you may believe that Jesus is the Christ, the Son of God; and that believing you may have life in His name* (John 20:31).

Just hearing or reading the Word is not enough; you must meditate on it and let the Holy Spirit make it real so that you can apply it to your life. Many people, even unbelievers, know something about the Word of God, but they don't know the power of His Word and how it can change their lives.

Whether you realize it or not, the Word of God brings forth fruit in your life. It is impossible for God's Word to lie dormant, inactive, and unproductive. When you plant seeds in good soil in your garden and carefully water, fertilize, and nurture them, they will grow and bear fruit! This is a law of nature as well as a law of God:

> *And the one on whom seed was sown on the good soil, this is the man who hears the word and understands it; who indeed bears fruit and brings forth, some a hundredfold, some sixty, and some thirty* (Matthew 13:23).

Your heavenly Father says "yes" to His promises. When you rely on His Word, He will honor His Word in your life. It could not be any simpler. When you place your confidence in God He will reward your trust every time:

> *For as many as are the promises of God, in Him they are yes; therefore also through Him is our Amen to the glory of God through us* (2 Corinthians 1:20).

As you begin to personalize God's Word by reading, meditating, and speaking it into your life, the character of Christ begins to develop in you:

> *For by these He has granted to us His precious and magnificent promises, so that by them you may become partakers of the divine nature* (2 Peter 1:4).

Although all of God's promises are yours, they are conditional based upon your faith. You must mix the Word of God with your faith in order for it to operate in your life. The power is in the Word, but it is your faith that *activates* that power:

> *For indeed we have had good news preached to us, just as they also; but the word they heard did not profit them, because it was not united by faith in those who heard* (Hebrews 4:2).

Remember, it was through faith that Abraham and Sarah received God's promise:

> *For the promise to Abraham or to his descendants that he would be heir of the world was not through the Law, but through the righteousness of faith* (Romans 4:13).

Even Jesus, the Son of God, could not use the healing promises of God where there was not an atmosphere of faith and belief:

> *And He was not able to do even one work of power there, except that He laid His hands on a few sickly people [and] cured them. And He marveled because of their unbelief (their lack of faith in Him)* (Mark 6:5–6 AMP).

Walk Your Talk

Faith without action is useless because if we talk about our faith but do not act on what we believe, we accomplish nothing. James said, *"Even so faith, if it has no works, is dead, being by itself"* (James 2:17).

Although James was talking specifically about good works toward others being a demonstration of genuine faith, the principle still holds true. "Faith" that is only talk and not borne out in our lifestyle is not true faith. Genuine faith—faith that gets results—is faith that is put into action.

Rahab the harlot is a perfect example of someone who placed her faith in God as the Lord of heaven and earth, followed through with action based on her faith, and got the result she wanted. Her story is recorded in the book of Joshua. A resident of the city of Jericho, Rahab had heard of the power of the God of Israel in defeating other enemies. She knew that the Israelites were headed for Jericho and that God had given the city into their hands. When two Israelite spies showed up in the city, she saw her opportunity and took it.

> *But the woman* [Rahab] *had taken the two men and hidden them....Before the two men had lain down, Rahab came up to them on the roof. And she said to the men, I know that the Lord has given you the land and that your terror is fallen upon us and that all the inhabitants of the land faint because of you....Now then, I pray you, swear to me by the Lord, since I have shown you kindness, that you also will show kindness to my father's house, and give me a sure sign, and save alive my father and mother, my brothers and sisters, and all they have, and deliver us from death* (Joshua 2:4, 8–9, 12–13 AMP).

Rahab was concerned not only with her own safety, but also that of her immediate family. She pleaded that they be spared too when the Israelites took the city. The spies agreed, and before they left, helped her devise a plan. They told her to hang a scarlet cord from her window as a marker. That red cord became the symbol of her hope and the guarantee of her salvation. By hanging the cord in her window, Rahab demonstrated her faith in the word of the spies that, by extension, was the promise of God.

Because of the faith and hope she placed in her newfound God, combined with her specific and deliberate action in response to her faith, Rahab and her entire household were saved when the Israelites captured and destroyed Jericho. As an added blessing, Rahab later married an Israelite and became a "blessed one." She was the mother of

Boaz and the great-great grandmother of King David, making her a direct lineal ancestor of the Lord Jesus Christ Himself.

The lesson of Rahab's life is clear: *Faith put into action works every time!* It is one thing to *say* we believe, but quite another to put feet to our profession. If our faith is genuine, it will show itself in our actions. *Actions demonstrate trust.*

Children do not have to see before they believe. They simply trust that what they are told is the truth, and they put their trust into action. A child will jump into his daddy's arms on nothing more than the promise that his daddy will catch him. There is no debate or question about it.

"Faith put into action works every time!"

That is the same way you should approach God with your faith. Even when physical evidence is lacking, you should simply take God at His word and press on. If your faith is in the "incubation" period, continue to nurture it patiently and in time you will reap the promised harvest. Continue to walk, talk, and live by faith—whether you see anything happening or not—knowing that the foundation of your faith, God Himself, is infinitely trustworthy.

STEPS TO A SIMPLER FAITH

1. Write down examples of when your faith may have been:

   Human

   Religious

   Experiential

   Intellectual

   Temporary

2. After you have searched the Word for promises concerning your situation, fuse your hope with faith! Share your hope with another person.

3. If you have been praying for a long time for something and haven't seen the answer, apply God's Word to the situation until you see it change!
4. Ask God to help you speak only positive, faith-filled words. Record these words in your journal or Scripture notebook.
5. List some of God's promises and ask Him to help you understand their place in your personal "faith walk."

CHAPTER TWO

The Gift That Keeps on Giving

How much faith does it take to get results? Peter Pan tells the Darling children that they can fly if they *believe strongly enough* (and have fairy dust, of course!). In other words, they will be able to fly if they *have enough faith*. Have you ever tried to believe God for something but didn't get an answer? Maybe you or someone close to you was sick and you prayed and believed for healing, yet healing did not come. Perhaps you or someone you know went through a major financial or emotional crisis and although you prayed for relief, things only seemed to get worse. During any such time in your life, has some well-meaning fellow believer ever said to you, "Well, God will work this out for you if you have *enough faith*"?

One of the ways we as Christians complicate the faith issue is by getting caught up in the question of quantity. How much faith is "enough" faith? Many believers live discouraged and defeated lives because they assume that the apparent absence of results in their lives is due to the fact that they do not have "enough" faith, whatever that means. Are you one of them? Do you sometimes wonder if you have enough faith to receive God's promises? Does it seem at times as though you have very little faith or even none at all?

If so, I have good news for you! Regardless of how "faith-less" you may feel or how spiritually unsuccessful your life appears to be, if you have been born again by the Spirit of God, *you have faith*! As a matter of fact, you have enough faith to get everything that God has for you and more. Paul said, *"God has allotted to each a measure of faith"* (Romans 12:3).

How much faith is "enough"? Very little, according to Jesus:

> *Truly I say to you, if you have faith the size of a mustard seed, you will say to this mountain, "Move from here to there," and it will move; and nothing will be impossible to you* (Matthew 17:20).

Faith the size of a tiny mustard seed is enough to move a mountain. Is it possible? In another place, Jesus spoke again about a mustard seed:

> *The kingdom of heaven is like a mustard seed, which a man took and sowed in his field; and this is smaller than all other seeds, but when it is full grown, it is larger than the garden plants and becomes a tree, so that the birds of the air come and nest in its branches* (Matthew 13:31–32).

Even though here Jesus is talking about the kingdom of heaven, there is a principle we can apply to faith. The mustard seed is the smallest of all seeds, yet it grows into the largest plant in the garden. In the same way, faith begins small, but over time, when properly nurtured, grows into greatness. *Faith is a growth process.*

> "Faith is a growth process."

Take a moment and think about the great people of faith in the Bible. Now think about someone you know whose strong faith you admire. Do you think any of these people had great faith right off the bat? No! Like all the rest of us, they began with a little bit of faith that, as they exercised and nurtured it, went through a normal growth pattern, slowly matured, and finally reached a state of greatness. If faith is simple enough for a child to understand, then even a child can have great faith. It doesn't take anyone special or super-gifted. Faith that gets results—mountain-moving faith—is available to anyone, *including you*.

The eleventh chapter of Hebrews is sometimes called "The Faith Hall of Fame" because it lists the names and exploits of some of the greatest people of faith in the Bible. One interesting fact that emerges in reading this "roll call of the faithful" is that nowhere is any mention made of their flaws, weaknesses, or errors. Only their great faith is cited. It used to bother me that God told us only about the mighty exploits of Abel, Enoch,

Noah, Abraham, Sarah, Moses, and all the others in Hebrews 11 without sharing any of their failures. Surely they didn't come into perfect faith without making mistakes along the way!

One day I complained to the Lord, "God, You're not telling us the whole story; You tell us only about their faith." Then I heard Him speak to me very clearly, "That's right, because I have forgotten everything they repented of." The same is true for you. God has forgiven and forgotten everything you have repented of because it is His will to do so. What God remembers about you is your faith because faith pleases Him. Isn't it wonderful that God forgets about our sins and remembers our faith?

Get Into the Word

Do you desire stronger faith but wonder how to get it? The only way you can continually move in faith is to become a diligent student of God's Word. There is no other path to faith: *"Faith comes by hearing, and hearing by the word of God"* (Romans 10:17 NKJV). The closer you get to Jesus and the more you really know Him, the stronger your faith will grow.

How do you get to know Jesus better? Learn His Word! Go straight to the source! As you see what He teaches about life situations, and as you make Him your faith source, you will be able to walk through all circumstances confident in Him. If you make Jesus the focal point of your faith walk, He will mature and perfect your faith.

> *Looking away [from all that will distract] to Jesus, Who is the Leader and the Source of our faith [giving the first incentive for our belief] and is also its Finisher, [bringing it to maturity and perfection]* (Hebrews 12:2 AMP).

Being born of God makes you a child of God, so your new nature is a faith nature. All children have the nature of their parents. Since God is a faith God, it is normal that His children be faith children, filled with His kind of faith. *"And Jesus answered saying to them, 'Have faith in God' "* (Mark 11:22). Some scholars translate this as, "Have the God-kind of faith." It is God's will and pleasure that we walk in His kind of powerful, mountain-moving faith. That kind of faith comes only by *knowing* and *living* the Word of God.

If you want a strong faith, a childlike faith that trusts the Lord implicitly and gets results, commit yourself to spend a great deal of time in God's Word—*every day*. You may be thinking, "But I'm too busy!" We all are busy these days, between job and family and all the other demands made on our attention. Sometimes it seems impossible to squeeze in anything else. The truth is, no matter how busy we are, we always somehow find the time for the things that are most important to us. If growing a strong faith is important enough to you, you will find the time to get into the Word of God. You may have to alter your schedule or even give up some things that are not as important, but your efforts will be well rewarded.

Make every effort to arrange your daily schedule around the Word because receiving God's Word into your spirit is the most important thing you can do. There are any number of practical ways to redeem or buy back time for God's Word that has been stolen by other affairs of life. If you are cooking or ironing or even taking a relaxing bath, listen to a tape of the recorded New Testament. When you are running errands or commuting to work, listen to a Bible tape or CD while you drive. You'll be surprised how much of the Word you can put in your spirit this way. Don't neglect these opportunities to buy back time and grow in faith through the Word of God!

If you are not already doing so, set aside a specific time each day—even if it is only ten or fifteen minutes—to focus exclusively on Bible reading and prayer. I know that doesn't sound like much, but you'll be amazed at how rich those ten minutes a day will become for you. Before long, you will find yourself wanting to take more time because you are so hungry for the Word and for the Lord's presence.

Faith comes by hearing, and hearing by the Word of God. Another way to enhance your "hearing" is to read the Bible aloud whenever possible. This gives you double hearing—your natural ear as well as your inner or spiritual ear.

Logos and *Rhema*

The Word of God relates to us in two specific ways. First, there is *logos*, a Greek word used to refer to the whole, revealed Word of God; in other words, the Bible as a whole. *Logos* signifies the "revealed will of God," as well as "a direct revelation given by Christ." It also represents the "personal manifestation...of the whole deity."[3] This is the word that John uses in the first chapter of his Gospel to refer to Jesus, who is the ultimate expression of God's Word, the *living* Word of God:

> *In the beginning was the Word* [logos], *and the Word* [logos] *was with God, and the Word* [logos] *was God....And the Word* [logos] *became flesh, and dwelt among us, and we saw His glory, glory as of the only begotten from the Father, full of grace and truth* (John 1:1, 14).

God also speaks to us with a *rhema* Word, which is a singular or specific Word that God speaks to us from the context of His overall Word (*logos*) for a specific situation. *Rhema* refers to "the individual scripture which the Spirit brings to our remembrance for use in time of need."[4] One example is found in Ephesians 6:17: *"And take the helmet of salvation, and the sword of the Spirit, which is the word* [rhema] *of God."* Here Paul was referring to specific Scriptures that the Spirit will remind us of to help us fight off attacks from the enemy.

You can use the Word to fight and defeat your foe, the devil. When you fill your heart with the whole *logos*, you build a reserve from which the Holy Spirit can bring to your remembrance a specific *rhema* for your situation. Don't feel that you need to bring the entire Bible against him—the Holy Spirit will bring to your remembrance a Scripture for that exact time and need. That is why it is absolutely necessary to regularly store the Word in your mind, for the Spirit can't bring it to remembrance if it's not there! As you learn to speak *rhema* into your circumstances, you will see things start to change and your faith will grow.

Jesus said, *"It is written, 'Man shall not live on bread alone, but on every word* [rhema] *that proceeds out of the mouth of God' "* (Matthew 4:4). We are to live by the *rhema* of God, but that starts by knowing the *logos*. The *logos* (the whole Word of God) forms the larger picture, but the guidance we receive on an everyday basis comes through the *rhema* of God.

Sometimes when you are walking by faith, the Holy Spirit will drop into your spirit a special kind of *rhema*, a special "gift of faith" to enable you to carry out a specific task. You may have a burden to see one particular person saved, or for someone to be healed or delivered, or for some other need to be met. This special "gift of faith" will fill you with a rock-solid certainty that the thing for which you are praying and believing God *will* come to pass. There will be absolutely no doubt in your mind.

I believe that Queen Esther in the Old Testament operated in this kind of "revelation faith" when she spoke out boldly and rescued her people. A Jewish woman who became queen of Persia, she was in a unique position to save her people from an insidious plot to destroy them. At the risk of her own life, she took a stand and brought deliverance. At one point she said, in essence, "If I perish, I perish, but I'm going to save my people" (Esther 4:16, paraphrased). Was she afraid? Probably, but she overcame her fear and stood courageously because she knew she had heard from God.

How does *rhema* Word work? How can you apply the Word of God to specific situations in your life? Here are some examples to give you an idea:

1. When you need assurance that your prayers will be answered:

   If you abide in Me, and My words abide in you, ask whatever you wish, and it will be done for you (John 15:7).

2. When you need reassurance that your sins have been forgiven:

   For the law of the Spirit of life in Christ Jesus has set you free from the law of sin and of death (Romans 8:2).

3. When you need healing:

   He sent His word and healed them, and delivered them from their destructions (Psalm 107:20).

4. When you have physical needs or suffer a financial setback:

   The young lions lack and suffer hunger; but those who seek the LORD shall not lack any good thing (Psalm 34:10 NKJV).

5. When you encounter opposition while trying to live according to God's will:

   Commit your works to the LORD, and your thoughts will be established (Proverbs 16:3 NKJV).

6. When you are engaged in spiritual warfare:

> *Behold, I give you the authority to trample on serpents and scorpions, and over all the power of the enemy, and nothing shall by any means hurt you* (Luke 10:19 NKJV).

Here are a few more Scriptures you may wish to memorize and personalize so that they will be in your spirit ready for you to confess for situations that arise:

> *The LORD is my shepherd, I shall not want* (Psalm 23:1).
>
> [I] *do not fear, for* [You are with me; I] *do not anxiously look about* [me], *for* [You are my] *God.* [You] *will strengthen* [me], *surely* [You] *will help* [me], *surely* [You] *will uphold* [me] *with* [Your] *righteous right hand* (Isaiah 41:10).
>
> *What then shall we say to these things? If God is for* [me], *who is against* [me]*?* (Romans 8:31)
>
> *I can do all things through Him who strengthens me* (Philippians 4:13).
>
> *The LORD is my light and my salvation; whom shall I fear? The LORD is the defense of my life; whom shall I dread?* (Psalm 27:1)
>
> *And my God will supply all* [my] *needs according to His riches in glory in Christ Jesus* (Philippians 4:19).
>
> *My help comes from the LORD, who made heaven and earth* (Psalm 121:2).

Listen, Learn, and Grow

Although it is important to *hear* the Word of God, it is even more important to *listen* to what we hear; otherwise the Word will not make any difference in our lives. *Listening* leads to *understanding*, understanding leads to *believing*, and believing leads to *doing*. James said, "*Be doers of the word, and not hearers only, deceiving yourselves*" (James 1:22 NKJV). If all we do is hear the Word and we never let it into our inner spirit, nothing will change. Learning to listen will open up the way for the Spirit to minister the Word in our hearts. It would be hard to underestimate the importance of listening for the growth of our faith. Jesus specifically instructed us to be good listeners:

> *So take care how you listen; for whoever has, to him more shall be given; and whoever does not have, even what he thinks he has shall be taken away from him* (Luke 8:18).

Jesus spoke these words right after He finished explaining the parable of the sower and the seed (see Luke 8:11–18). Four kinds of "ground" received (heard) the "seed" of God's Word, but only one—the "good" ground—took it to heart and bore fruit. The other three—the wayside, the rocky, and the thorny ground—never bore fruit because they never allowed the Word to penetrate deep inside. The "good" ground, on the other hand, heard the Word in an honest and good heart and held it fast. This was not passive hearing, but active listening that brought a positive response! Listening to the Word and then doing it is what made the good ground successful and fruitful.

Failure to listen can lead to deception. When Isaac, Abraham's son, was old and blind, he was deceived into giving his youngest son, Jacob, the blessing that should have gone to Esau, his firstborn son. Jacob, who was smooth-skinned, disguised himself with animal skins so he would feel hairy like his brother Esau. Then he went into Isaac and greeted his father. Had Isaac *listened* to what his ears were telling him, he would not have been fooled by Jacob's deception:

> *Then Isaac said to Jacob, "Please come close, that I may feel you, my son, whether you are really my son Esau or not." So Jacob came close to Isaac his father, and he felt him and said, "The voice is the voice of Jacob, but the hands are the hands of Esau." He did not recognize him, because his hands were hairy like his brother Esau's hands; so he blessed him* (Genesis 27:21–23).

Likewise, if we fail to *listen* to the Word of God when we hear it, we will fail to understand it and may make ourselves vulnerable to being deceived by the enemy. *Listening* to the Word of God is *vital*.

The ability to really listen helped a woman in the New Testament receive healing for a sickness that had plagued her for years:

> *A woman who had had a hemorrhage for twelve years, and had endured much at the hands of many physicians, and had spent all that she had and was not helped at all, but rather had grown worse—after hearing about Jesus, she came up in the crowd behind Him and touched His cloak. For she thought, "If I just touch His garments, I will get well." Immediately the flow of her blood was dried up; and she felt in her body that she was healed of her affliction* (Mark 5:25–29).

This woman was ill, getting worse, and desperate. Then she *heard* about Jesus and His healing power. Rather than letting things rest there, she put *action* to what she heard. In other words, she *listened* to what she heard and understood that Jesus could help her. Her faith gave her the courage to move through the crowd and touch the hem of Jesus' garment, even though her condition made her unclean under the law, which prohibited her from touching anyone.

> "Listening to the Word of God is vital."

A spirit of faith was loosed in this woman and she said, "If I can touch His clothes, I will be healed." One translation from the Greek explains that she kept saying over and over, "I will be made whole; I will be made whole; I will be made whole." Her objective was simple—getting healed—and as she focused on that objective, speaking it over and over, her faith grew and bore fruit. She was made whole and completely clean because she *listened* when she heard about Jesus.

A similar act of listening that brought great results is recorded in the fourteenth chapter of Acts, where Paul was preaching in the city of Lystra:

> *At Lystra a man was sitting who had no strength in his feet, lame from his mother's womb, who had never walked. This man was listening to Paul as he spoke, who, when he had fixed his gaze on him and had seen that he had faith to be made well, said with a loud voice, "Stand upright on your feet." And he leaped up and began to walk* (Acts 14:8–10).

Paul was preaching the Gospel and this lame man was *listening*. At some point, the man perceived that the Christ whom Paul preached had the power to heal him, and faith bloomed in his heart. When Paul told the man to stand up, he acted on his faith, stood up, and received total healing.

Listening to the Word of God in order to grow our faith involves more than hearing with our ears; it means listening with our *heart*. The heart, of course, is the primary organ of physical life. It pumps blood throughout the body, and blood is vital to the life of the body. Leviticus 17:11 says, *"For the life of the flesh is in the blood."* In ancient times, the heart was believed to be the center not only of physical life but also of thoughts and emotions. Over time, the word *heart* came to stand for man's entire mental and moral activity, both the rational and the emotional elements. Just as the heart occupies the most important place in human physiology, so also in a figurative sense it is central to our emotional and spiritual life.

Simple, God-pleasing faith that will change your life will always come through your heart, or spirit, rather than through your five senses. Your senses are the gateway through which the Word enters when you first hear it, but it is your heart that brings your faith to life. Peter called the human spirit *"the hidden person of the heart"* (1 Peter 3:4). In Romans 7:22, Paul called it *"the inner man."* The "heart" is where you believe, the part of you where faith takes place:

> *If you confess with your mouth Jesus as Lord, and believe in your heart that God raised Him from the dead, you will be saved; for with the heart a person believes, resulting in righteousness, and with the mouth he confesses, resulting in salvation* (Romans 10:9–10).

Your faith can grow continually because your "inner man" is re-created and renewed daily:

> *Therefore we do not lose heart, but though our outer man is decaying, yet our inner man is being renewed day by day* (2 Corinthians 4:16).

> *That He would grant you, according to the riches of His glory, to be strengthened with power through His Spirit in the inner man, so that Christ may dwell in your hearts through faith* (Ephesians 3:16–17).

There are times when our hearts receive God's truth even when our minds cannot grasp it. In fact, many times our minds can actually hinder our comprehension! Thankfully, we have the Holy Spirit to help our minds understand what our hearts have readily received from God:

> *For to us God revealed them through the Spirit; for the Spirit searches all things, even the depths of God....But a natural man does not accept the things of the Spirit of God, for they are foolishness to him; and he cannot understand them, because they are spiritually appraised* (1 Corinthians 2:10, 14).

> *But when He, the Spirit of truth, comes, He will guide you into all the truth; for He will not speak on His own initiative, but whatever He hears, He will speak; and He will disclose to you what is to come* (John 16:13).

Let the Holy Spirit teach you through the Word, for as the Word feeds your spirit, your faith will grow!

Meditate Day and Night

Another important way of getting the Word into our heart and mind is by learning to meditate on it. For many Christians today, meditation is an unknown art. Much has been said and written about meditation, in both the secular and spiritual worlds. Because of this, many believers are confused or uncertain about meditation. Since much of the secular world practices meditation in ungodly ways, it is important that we understand what it means from the perspective of God's Word.

To meditate means to reflect or contemplate or ponder over something. The New Testament Greek word for "meditate," *meletao*, also means "ponder, imagine, attend to, practice, to care for."[5] This is the same action as worrying, only in reverse! Another word that captures the idea of what it means to meditate is *ruminate*, in the sense of contemplating something slowly and carefully.

Anyone who knows anything about cows knows that they are ruminants. This means that they chew the cud. Like most other ruminants, a cow has four stomachs. As a cow chews and swallows its food, the food goes into the rumen, the first of the cow's four stomachs, where initial digestion occurs. Then the cow regurgitates the partially digested food into its mouth again, where it chews some more, then swallows. Each time, the food passes successively through each stomach and back up to be chewed again before being swallowed the final time. Every time the cow chews its cud it gleans more nutrition from its food.

In this same way, we need to "chew" on the Word of God. We need to "masticate" the Word—ruminate, contemplate, and ponder over it. That is what it means to meditate on God's Word. There are several ways to do this. Perhaps the best way is to read a portion of God's Word, perhaps only a verse or two, then ponder over it several times throughout the day. Say it over and over again, asking God to reveal truth from it. Turn it around, take it apart, and memorize it. Personalize the verse by applying it to your present situation, then visualize the Word coming to pass in your life. Like a cow chewing its cud, the more you "ruminate" on the Word, the more nutrition you will glean from it as the Holy Spirit continues to reveal new truths to you. The more spiritual truth you learn from God's Word, the more your faith will grow.

"We need to 'chew' on the Word of God."

My husband tells about an elderly relative who lived near him while he was growing up. This man would sit in his rocking chair on the front porch, rocking back and forth and repeating, "I wish I had a million dollars. I wish I had a million dollars. I wish I had a million dollars." That old man made a lasting impression on my husband. Even as a young child he could see that wishing did not always get you what you wanted. *Wishing* for prosperity will not make it happen. If you wish to prosper in faith and in life, set your mind and heart to *learn* God's Word and then *speak* and *act* upon it!

This is the lesson that Joshua had to learn. After Moses died, Joshua faced the difficult task of leading the Israelites into the Promised Land. Accomplishing this assignment required great faith and courage on Joshua's part. God told him to have courage, but He also gave him specific instructions to help him prepare. Part of Joshua's preparation was learning to meditate on God's Word:

> *This book of the law shall not depart from your mouth, but you shall meditate on it day and night, so that you may be careful to do according to all that is written in it; for then you will make your way prosperous, and then you will have success* (Joshua 1:8).

This verse contains three keys to prosperity and success: keep the Word in your mouth (speak it over and over), meditate on the Word (keep it in your mind), and obey the Word (keep it in your life). Joshua did all of these things and God enabled him to lead Israel to victory.

Meditation is one of the God-ordained ways for us to get His Word deeply into our spirit. Like Joshua, if we speak the Word with our mouths, ponder it in our hearts, and obey it in our lives, we too will prosper in every way. That is God's promise:

> *How blessed is the man who does not walk in the counsel of the wicked, nor stand in the path of sinners, nor sit in the seat of scoffers! But his delight is in the law of the* Lord*, and in His law he meditates day and night. He will be like a tree firmly planted by streams of water, which yields its fruit in its season and its leaf does not wither; and in whatever he does, he prospers* (Psalm 1:1–3).

These are marvelous promises! If you are faithful to the Lord and in meditating on His Word, He will bless you, plant (establish) you firmly, nourish you, and make you fruitful and prosperous. Faith that grows from intimate knowledge of God's Word will cause you to excel. What more do you need?

Faith and Love

Once you have firmly established your faith with God's Word, you can begin using it to receive the promises of God. Remember, His promises are obtained by faith. Perhaps you already have known the promises of God, confessed them, accepted them, and even received answers to some of your prayers. That's wonderful! Even with that, however, your faith can waver if you confess something for a long time and nothing happens. What do you do then? The Lord wants you to stand firm:

> *Let us hold fast the confession of our hope without wavering, for He who promised is faithful* (Hebrews 10:23).

> *My son, give attention to my words; incline your ear to my sayings. Do not let them depart from your sight; keep them in the midst of your heart. For they are life to those who find them and health to all their body* (Proverbs 4:20–22).

Hold fast to your confession and keep God's Word in the midst of your heart. In other words, be a bulldog about your faith. Don't let go no matter what.

Part of holding fast your confession is to give regular expression to your faith. Strong faith needs to be coupled with action, and expressing your faith not only communicates it to others, but also strengthens it in you. Speaking your faith will cause it to grow and multiply in your life and in the lives of others. By the same token, if you are always speaking your doubts and fears, those will multiply instead. Stop speaking your doubts and keep speaking your faith. Don't let your words become more important than God's words.

"Be a bulldog about your faith."

If you are confessing something in faith and have gone a long time with no answer, you may need to examine your love quotient. No believer should seek to become a person of great faith without also seeking to love much because faith works by love. In fact, without love, faith cannot work. The Bible makes it clear that without love, all the gifts, talent, and faith in the world are worthless:

> *If I speak with the tongues of men and of angels, but do not have love, I have become a noisy gong or a clanging cymbal. If I have the gift of prophecy, and know all mysteries and all knowledge; and if I have all faith, so as to remove mountains, but do not have love, I am nothing. And if I give all my possessions to feed the poor, and if I surrender my body to be burned, but do not have love, it profits me nothing* (1 Corinthians 13:1–3).

Kenneth Hagin, Jr. has said, "If we are to live in line with God's Word, we must not only be the faith child of a faith God, but we must be the love child of a love God." Faith and love go together. When James said that faith without works is dead, the "works" he had in mind were good deeds we do for others as acts and expressions of our love—in other words, *faith and love in action*. In his prayer of thanks for the Thessalonian believers, Paul also linked faith and love: *"We give thanks to God always for all of you, making mention of you in our prayers; constantly bearing in mind your **work of faith** and **labor of love** and steadfastness of hope in our Lord Jesus Christ in the presence of our God and Father"* (1 Thessalonians 1:2–3, emphasis added).

Have you ever shared the Gospel of Christ with a person and told that person about the indescribable love of Jesus? Talking about God's love can remind us again of how wonderful it is to know Him and make us want to please Him in everything we do. If you have an intimate relationship with Jesus and let His love live in you, you will have the kind of faith that can move mountains! Set yourself to become equally a child of faith and a child of love because your heavenly Father is the author of both!

Sink Your Roots Deep

Children generally share many characteristics of their parents. As children of God in Christ, we share His nature and are members of His family. One essential thing that children share with their parents is a *personal relationship*. Likewise, childlike, God-pleasing faith is *personal* faith. If you want a faith that really works in your life, that faith *must* be *personal*. The faith you rely upon *must* be your own. Do not become dependent upon the personal faith of a pastor, a teacher, a friend, a family member, or anyone else. Faith by proxy simply won't cut it. Secondhand faith will not work. It has been said that God has no grandchildren—only children. He wants you to be firmly established in your own faith:

> "The faith you rely upon must be your own."

> *Therefore as you have received Christ Jesus the Lord, so walk in Him, having been firmly rooted and now being built up in Him and established in your faith, just as you were instructed, and overflowing with gratitude* (Colossians 2:6–7).

Although we cannot make another's faith our own, we can learn from the example of others. I learned about faith from my mother, who was a mighty woman of the Word. One of the most important things she taught me was the value and power of *speaking* my faith.

My mother became Spirit-filled while I was away at college. One weekend I came home to find that everything had changed! Bibles were on the end tables, our home had been transformed in many other ways, and my mother was like a different person, completely turned on for Jesus. At the time, I knew nothing about this "Spirit-filled" life and it was rather confusing to me.

We had a large cottonwood tree in our yard. Our next-door neighbors had one, too. Separated only by a fence, those cottonwood trees were so close together that they looked like one tree. Both were plagued with an infestation of nasty, hideous worms. These worms would eat leaves and then drop a little thread-like substance afterwards. They were not at all discriminating in where they dropped it, either! If any of us stood under the trees, we could easily end up with worm droppings in our hair. When we walked under the trees, our feet would "squish" in the droppings on the ground. It was dreadful!

My mother wanted my father to spray our tree, but he felt it was too expensive. He also told her, "I know the neighbors are having their tree sprayed, but those worms have eggs, and they'll hatch and then there will be more worms. It's just money down the drain." Nothing my mother said could persuade him.

Mother was determined to get rid of those worms, and now she had a new weapon in her arsenal: faith! One day she declared, "I'm going out there and curse those worms in the name of Jesus. They're on my tree on my property, and I'm going to tell them to get off, in Jesus' name!"

I was horrified. "Mother, surely you're not going to do that in broad daylight!"

Her boldness shocked me. Walking right out to our tree in the middle of the day, she cursed those worms in the name of Jesus and demanded that they never come back. The next day we walked out into the backyard and the ground was really squishy. Not only were there worm droppings, but all the worms were on the ground, as well. They had fallen out of the tree—dead!

Over the next several days we watched our neighbors' tree and observed a very interesting thing. They killed the worms with spray, but their eggs still hatched. New worms came out and continued to do damage, just as my father had predicted. Despite the closeness of the two trees, however, the worms from their tree never came over and bothered our tree. I believe they didn't dare cross over and touch our tree because my mother had cursed them in the name of Jesus—and Jesus' name gives you dominion.

My mother spoke and "established" that our tree was protected by the name of Jesus. You also can establish a thing by speaking it out loud in agreement with God's Word. That is how you were saved—you believed and then confessed Jesus as Savior and Lord. The word of faith should always be in your mouth:

> *But what does it say? "The word is near you, in your mouth and in your heart"—that is, the word of faith* (Romans 10:8).

When you confess the promises and blessings of God, you are claiming them as your own. God has given you a *"measure of faith,"* the *logos* of the Word, a will to choose, and a mouth with which to speak. The more you choose to speak the Word of God, the more it becomes yours. Once the Word of God becomes part of you, no one can take it away from you.

God and His Word cannot be separated. When you become one with God's Word, you become one with God. As you speak and confess His Word, God hears what you say and so do you. God is true to His Word and will bring it to pass in His good time. That which you constantly speak you eventually will believe, so keep speaking the Word of God. You will build up your faith and begin to see His Word working in your life.

"You eventually believe what you constantly speak."

When Sarah was in high school, she desperately wanted to be on the varsity basketball team. With this goal in mind, she began to practice hard, hour after hour. At the same time she began speaking words in faith, saying, "I am on the varsity team this year in school. I am going to be on the first-string varsity team." The more she said the words, the more she believed them in her heart and the more determined she became. In the end, she did make the varsity team and played very well!

Sarah also had a strong desire for good grades. Accordingly, she began to speak words of faith in that area as well. "I'm the head and not the tail. I have the mind of Christ in me." Every morning before Sarah walked out the door to catch her bus, she would say to me, "I am ten times wiser! I am wise because I have His wisdom." When she got her report card, she had straight A's except for one B!

Take some time to examine your own faith life. Remember, even "mustard-seed" faith is enough faith to make a difference if your trust is centered squarely on the Lord. Get into God's Word on a regular basis. Read it, memorize it, personalize it, and meditate on it. Learn to listen—*really* listen—to what the Holy Spirit is teaching you through the Word. Stop speaking negative words into your life and situation. Get in the habit of speaking faith, hope, and the Word of God over your circumstances instead. Speaking and confessing God's Word will release the spirit of faith into every area of your life. The more you speak, the more your faith will grow, and the more your faith grows, the more your life will change!

STEPS TO A SIMPLER FAITH

1. Help your faith grow by doing the following every day:

   Read the Word

   Confess the Word

   Memorize the Word

   Meditate on the Word

   Obey the Word

2. Study the difference between the words *logos* and *rhema* and explain them in your own words. Keep a list of personal "*rhema*" words that God gives to you through His Spirit.
3. Ask the Lord to help you personalize your faith through the Word. Follow the example of the following Scripture:

   He Himself bore [my] *sins in His body on the cross, so that* [I] *might die to sin and live to righteousness; for by His wounds* [I was] *healed* (1 Peter 2:24).

4. Meditate on how love affects faith by reading these verses:

   Galatians 5:6–14

   Ephesians 4:1–3

Ephesians 4:15, 29

Ephesians 5:1–2

5. Think of a person of "great faith" whom you know. What spiritual habits can you learn from this person that will help you in your own faith walk?

CHAPTER THREE

The Language of Faith

Have you ever considered how much power lies in the words you speak? Though it may not be visible to the naked eye like the immense torrent of Niagara Falls, great power resides in the spoken word—power for good or evil, power to unleash either positive or negative forces in your life and the lives of others.

The words we speak and the language we use have a tremendous influence over what happens in our lives. This influence begins at birth. The language children learn depends on their nationality and culture. Studies have shown that all babies are born with the capacity to learn and speak *any* language equally well, a capacity that normally fades with age. That is why children who move to another nation usually pick up the indigenous language more quickly and speak it more fluently than their parents do.

Children learn language by example as well as by instruction; it does not come automatically. In other words, our children will learn the language *we* teach them. The words they hear all the time are the words they will learn to speak. This goes far beyond the matter simply of learning English or Spanish or French. Children also will pick up the *attitude* and the *tone* of the language they hear. If they hear positive, affirming speech, then that is the speech they will learn. They will learn negative and condemning speech just as quickly if that is what fills their environment.

There are two forces at work in the spiritual realm: the *creative* power of God and the *destructive* power of Satan. The words we speak and the language we use will serve one or the other. We speak either creation or destruction, life or death. Our words will either build up or tear down, encourage or discourage, affirm or deny, embrace or reject, and feed belief or unbelief. Our faith will rise or fall on the words we speak. For this reason, it is vitally important that we learn to speak fluently the language of faith.

"Our faith will rise or fall on the words we speak."

The Bible clearly links faith with the creative speech of God:

> *By faith we understand that the worlds were prepared by the word of God, so that what is seen was not made out of things which are visible* (Hebrews 11:3).

God *"prepared"* or *created* the *"worlds"* by His word. This truth is found throughout the Scriptures:

> *By the word of the LORD the heavens were made, and by the breath of His mouth all their host....For He spoke, and it was done; He commanded, and it stood fast* (Psalm 33:6, 9).

As the book of Genesis reveals, God spoke the universe into existence. Ten times in the first chapter God released His faith through the creative power of His word. God's power is so awesome that all He had to do was speak, and matter was created out of nothing. Whenever God says something, it is so:

> *Then God said, "Let there be light"; and there was light....Then God said, "Let there be an expanse in the midst of the waters, and let it separate the waters from the waters."...and it was so....Then God said, "Let the earth sprout vegetation: plants yielding seed, and fruit trees on the earth bearing fruit after their kind with seed in them"; and it was so* (Genesis 1:3, 6, 7, 11).

Can you imagine having the power to speak things into being? The universe and everything in it was created by God's spoken word. Jesus

Christ, as the living Word of God, is the one through whom all things were made. Even today He sustains all things through the power of His Word:

> *God, after He spoke long ago to the fathers in the prophets in many portions and in many ways, in these last days has spoken to us in His Son, whom He appointed heir of all things, through whom also He made the world. And He is the radiance of His glory and the exact representation of His nature, and upholds all things by the word of His power* (Hebrews 1:1–3).

Standing in opposition to God and His creative Word is Satan with his speech of deceit and destruction. Satan, also called Lucifer in some Bible versions, was originally a powerful and beautiful angel with a place of high honor in heaven. The name *Lucifer* literally means "morning star." Based on Scriptures in Ezekiel, I believe he had a beautiful voice and took the praise that came up from the earth and spoke that praise to God:

> *You were in Eden, the garden of God...* ***the workmanship of your timbrels and pipes was prepared for you on the day you were created.*** *You were the anointed cherub who covers; I established you; you were on the holy mountain of God.... You were perfect in your ways from the day you were created, till iniquity was found in you* (Ezekiel 28:13–15 NKJV, emphasis added).

Lucifer was in a glorious position—until iniquity was found in him. Because of his beauty and high position, Lucifer became proud and arrogant. No longer satisfied with being a servant, he exalted himself, tried to steal the praise that belonged to God, and sought to establish his own throne in heaven.

Finally God said, "That's enough!" and cast Lucifer out of heaven:

> *How you are fallen from heaven, O Lucifer, son of the morning! How you are cut down to the ground, you who weakened the nations! For you have said in your heart: "I will ascend into heaven, I will exalt my throne above the stars of God; I will also sit on the mount of the congregation on the farthest sides of the north; I will ascend above the heights of the clouds, I will be like the Most High." Yet you shall be brought down to Sheol, to the lowest depths of the Pit* (Isaiah 14:12–15 NKJV).

Since the day he was cast out of heaven, Satan has existed with only one purpose—to influence others to rebel against the Most High God. Whenever Satan speaks, he speaks nothing but lies and deception. Throughout the ages his words have caused great damage and destruction.

The Tongue: A Dangerous Weapon

The words we speak reveal whose voice we are listening to: God's voice of creative good or Satan's voice of destructive evil. Part of growing in our faith as believers is learning to be consistent in our speech. If we want to be like our heavenly Father, we must learn to speak as He speaks. This means always speaking the truth, always speaking blessings and not curses, and always speaking in such a way as to build others up rather than tear them down.

Few people truly realize what a powerful weapon the tongue is. The tongue is a mighty force in our lives that we use either for good or evil. James minced no words when he warned about the power—and danger—of the tongue:

> *Now if we put the bits into the horses' mouths so that they will obey us, we direct their entire body as well. Look at the ships also, though they are so great and are driven by strong winds, are still directed by a very small rudder wherever the inclination of the pilot desires. So also the tongue is a small part of the body, and yet it boasts of great things. See how great a forest is set aflame by such a small fire! And the tongue is a fire, the very world of iniquity; the tongue is set among our members as that which defiles the entire body, and sets on fire the course of our life, and is set on fire by hell. For every species of beasts and birds, of reptiles and creatures of the sea, is tamed and has been tamed by the human race. But no one can tame the tongue; it is a restless evil and full of deadly poison. With it we bless our Lord and Father, and with it we curse men, who have been made in the likeness of God; from the same mouth come both blessing and cursing. My brethren, these things ought not to be this way* (James 3:3–10).

How well do you guard your speech? Just as a bit in the mouth of a horse guides him in the right direction and a small rudder steers a large ship, your tongue, small as it is, has the power to guide your words, thoughts, emotions, and body into paths of prosperity and success. On the other hand, it can just as easily destroy your physical body, your thought life, and your emotions and bring you to ruin. Corrupt words also can destroy those around you and cause lasting pain and devastation.

James said that the tongue is a fire that sets our lives on fire and is itself set on fire by hell. What this means is that if you are not careful, Satan will use your own tongue against you. Your negative words will become his weapons to bring about your defeat. If Satan controls your tongue, he controls your life!

"Be careful, or Satan will use your own tongue against you."

It does not have to be that way. The power of the tongue works in both directions. Just as Satan can use your tongue to defeat you, you can use your tongue to defeat him! Revelation 12:11 says that God's children overcome Satan by *"the blood of the Lamb"* and *"the word of their testimony."* You can overcome the enemy by using your powerful tongue against him, speaking the Word of the Lord over your life and into your situation and calling forth blessings and not curses.

Few of us get through life without having negative words spoken at some point against us or our loved ones. Have you ever wondered whether the negative confessions of others can curse your life? The answer is *no!* God's Word is explicit:

> *"No weapon that is formed against you will prosper; and every tongue that accuses you in judgment you will condemn. This is the heritage of the servants of the LORD, and their vindication is from Me," declares the LORD* (Isaiah 54:17).

Negative words make up one of Satan's most potent weapons against us. If someone has said something negative about you or if you have been falsely accused, don't try to fight in a natural way. Put your tongue to work speaking the Word of God and His promises into your situation. Combat Satan's lies with the Lord's truth. In the name of Jesus, condemn the *words* spoken against you. Be careful never to condemn the person who spoke them, only their words. Then their negative words cannot harm you.

Positive, godly words can comfort the sad, heal the brokenhearted, cool anger, and bring order to confusion. They can restore courage, calm the fearful, motivate right actions, and stop the wicked one. Good words can help heal the sick, release the imprisoned, and feed the poor. Learning to speak the right words will strengthen your faith and build up your life, bringing peace and contentment: *"With the fruit of a man's mouth his stomach will be satisfied; he will be satisfied with the product of his lips"* (Proverbs 18:20). Best of all, your words can announce God's Word and become a channel for His blessings to flow to others! Wise words rightly spoken can be more valuable than earthly treasures.

> *There is gold, and an abundance of jewels; but the lips of knowledge are a more precious thing* (Proverbs 20:15).

> *Like apples of gold in settings of silver is a word spoken in right circumstances. Like an earring of gold and an ornament of fine gold is a wise reprover to a listening ear* (Proverbs 25:11–12).

Watch Your Words

Our words reflect our character. Some people look righteous and holy—until they open their mouths! What you say is powerful because through your words you show the world what is in your heart. Jesus said:

> *The tree is known by its fruit. ...For the mouth speaks out of that which fills the heart. The good man brings out of his good treasure what is good; and the evil man brings out of his evil treasure what is evil* (Matthew 12:33–35).

The words we speak begin as thoughts in our minds. Our hearts shape the way we think and feel, and those thoughts and feelings come out in our words. That is why we must be very careful about what we say and about making sure that our words line up with our claim to be children of God:

> *But above all, my brethren, do not swear, either by heaven or by earth or with any other oath; but your yes is to be yes, and your no, no, so that you may not fall under judgment* (James 5:12).

> *But now you also, put them all aside: anger, wrath, malice, slander, and abusive speech from your mouth* (Colossians 3:8).

> *Let your speech always be with grace, as though seasoned with salt, so that you will know how you should respond to each person* (Colossians 4:6).

Our words also reveal our new nature in Christ. As we believe the Word, we should speak what we believe:

> *But having the same spirit of faith, according to what is written, "I believed, therefore I spoke," we also believe, therefore also we speak* (2 Corinthians 4:13).

Not long ago I was praying for a woman for the healing of her cancer. People would ask me how she was doing, and I would tell them that she wasn't doing very well. After I said that three or four times, I heard the Lord say in my spirit, "Don't say that. You don't have to say that she is not doing well. You can just say that the reports are not good, but that you are believing the Word." Saying that the woman was not doing well was getting into my heart and affecting my faith for her.

Your tongue is a powerful weapon. Use it to speak faith and healing and prosperity into your life. Use it to speak the Word of God!

When Jesus said that a tree is known by its fruit, He was not talking about horticulture but about human lives. Just as a diseased tree will produce bad fruit, so a corrupt heart will produce evil thoughts, words, and actions. On the other hand, a pure heart, like a healthy tree, will bring forth pure and healthy fruit: strong faith, wise and helpful words, and positive behavior.

Jesus also said that our words will either justify us or condemn us. In other words, God will hold us accountable for every word we speak:

> *But I tell you that every careless word that people speak, they shall give an accounting for it in the day of judgment. For by your words you will be justified, and by your words you will be condemned* (Matthew 12:36–37).

The Greek word for "careless" in verse 36 also means useless, lazy, idle, barren, and slow. Although profanity falls into this category, much more is involved. A careless word is anything we say that tears down someone else, such as hurtful words we say without thinking: "Can't you do *anything* right?" "You'll never amount to anything!" "You're hopeless!"

Careless words also include murmuring or complaining. I remember one night I was murmuring over a situation that was not to my liking. My son Mike said, "Mother, you say, 'What things you desire when you pray, believe that you receive them, and you shall have them.' Mother, have you *really* prayed about your need? If so, then don't you really believe that you will have it?"

Mike's words were like an arrow to my heart. Right there I repented to God and to my family for murmuring. Our tongue *does* control our attitude as well as our faith.

Self-control begins with our tongue. Careless words do incredible harm, and once spoken, are impossible to recall. That is why we must be so very careful to tame our tongues and watch our words. Sometimes controlling our tongue seems impossible and, in our own strength, it is. The good news, however, is that when we put forth the effort the Lord will help us. What we cannot do on our own, the Holy Spirit can do in us.

Guard the Gab

One of the most dangerous kinds of careless words is gossip. Gossip can destroy not only the life and reputation of the person being talked about, but also those of the person doing the talking as well. A gossip is someone who habitually reveals personal or sensational facts about others. Whether or not those "facts" are true is of no concern. For this reason, someone who spreads gossip reveals a basic lack of integrity. The harmful effects of gossip are well-known. For instance, gossip can destroy friendship:

> *He who conceals a transgression seeks love, but he who repeats a matter separates intimate friends* (Proverbs 17:9).

Have you ever thought that even some prayer requests might actually be gossip? "We need to really pray for Mary. I'm sure she wouldn't mind my sharing this with you...." Well, maybe she *would* mind! *Always* use discernment and weigh your motives very carefully before you share privileged information with anyone else. Gossip can cause strife and wreak all kinds of havoc, so be careful that you are not the one who adds fuel to the fire:

> *For lack of wood the fire goes out, and where there is no whisperer, contention quiets down. Like charcoal to hot embers and wood to fire, so is a contentious man to kindle strife* (Proverbs 26:20–21).

Gossip is serious business in God's eyes. His Word plainly warns us not to gossip or associate with those who do:

> *He who goes about as a slanderer reveals secrets, therefore do not associate with a gossip* (Proverbs 20:19).

Notice the close link in this verse between gossip and slander! There is very little difference between the two. Slander involves false charges or statements that defame and damage a person's reputation. Gossip does the same thing; the only difference is that with gossip, the statements may, in a strict sense, be "true." True or not, gossip talks about another person in such a manner as to place that person in an unfavorable light.

"Gossip is serious business in God's eyes."

The Word of God leaves no doubt about what our attitude should be regarding gossip and slander:

> *Let all bitterness and wrath and anger and clamor and slander be put away from you, along with all malice. Be kind to one another, tender-hearted, forgiving each other, just as God in Christ also has forgiven you* (Ephesians 4:31–32).

> *Therefore,* [put] *aside all malice and all deceit and hypocrisy and envy and all slander* (1 Peter 2:1).

> *For the one who desires life, to love and see good days, must keep his tongue from evil and his lips from speaking deceit* (1 Peter 3:10).

Closely related to gossip is speaking deceitful things—lies or half-truths:

> *Keep your tongue from evil and your lips from speaking deceit* (Psalm 34:13).

God's Word also warns us against speaking in a devious, conniving, or scheming way:

Put away from you a deceitful mouth and put devious speech far from you (Proverbs 4:24).

Flattery is a form of deceitful speech because it is insincere. We all love to receive compliments, and kind words can be very encouraging and uplifting, but watch out for flattery. Be careful not to speak insincerely to others, and be alert and discerning when others speak to you that way. Like gossip, slander, and deceitful words, flattery can destroy lives:

A lying tongue hates those it crushes, and a flattering mouth works ruin (Proverbs 26:28).

The one who guards his mouth preserves his life; the one who opens wide his lips comes to ruin (Proverbs 13:3).

Help, LORD, for the godly man ceases to be, for the faithful disappear from among the sons of men. They speak falsehood to one another; with flattering lips and with a double heart they speak. May the LORD cut off all flattering lips, the tongue that speaks great things (Psalm 12:1–3).

Perhaps you are confident that you never do any of these things, but be on guard against pride. Proverbs 16:18 (NKJV) says, *"Pride goes before destruction, and a haughty spirit before a fall."* Unless you remain constantly alert to what and how you speak, you will very likely fall into the trap of speaking negative words. Gossip can be very subtle, so examine your motives carefully on a daily basis.

Some years ago we had a difficult situation arise when a staff member began speaking against my leadership. Despite being corrected, his negativity continued. I was tempted to speak back in a negative way, but God showed me that returning evil for evil would never change the situation. Instead, I began to speak goods things about the man. He did not change immediately, but at the end of six months, we experienced a miracle. This man is now my friend. The Bible says that when our ways please the Lord, He makes even our enemies to be at peace with us (see Proverbs 16:7).

Loose Lips Sink Ships

Careless words also include much of the joking and storytelling that has become so prevalent in our culture, particularly in the entertainment industry. Not all joking and silly talk is harmless, so we must set careful limits on how far we go in our story and joke telling. Paul was quite blunt on this matter:

> *But immorality or any impurity or greed must not even be named among you, as is proper among saints; and there must be no filthiness and silly talk, or coarse jesting, which are not fitting, but rather giving of thanks* (Ephesians 5:3–4).

Through the years, it seems that Christians in general have become much more accepting of profanity and immorality on television, the movie screen, and in literature, as well as dirty jokes and off-color stories from comics. This is partly due to changes in our culture. As Christians, however, we are not to be guided by our culture, which is constantly changing, but by the Word of God, which never changes.

During World War II, the Americans on the home front were cautioned against speaking too freely in public because they might unwittingly provide useful information to enemy spies. One slogan that became well-known in this regard was, "Loose lips sink ships." It meant that someone's unguarded speech could lead to disaster. That same principle applies to our own lives today. God's Word cautions us to guard our words carefully and not be too hasty in our speaking. Self-control is very important:

> *When there are many words, transgression is unavoidable, but he who restrains his lips is wise* (Proverbs 10:19).

> *Do you see a man who is hasty in his words? There is more hope for a fool than for him* (Proverbs 29:20).

> *Words from the mouth of a wise man are gracious, while the lips of a fool consume him; the beginning of his talking is folly and the end of it is wicked madness. Yet the fool multiplies words. No man knows what will happen, and who can tell him what will come after him?* (Ecclesiastes 10:12–14)

There are many ways our tongue can trip us up. We cannot afford to drop our guard for a moment. Only by yielding our hearts and minds continually to the Spirit of God can we avoid speaking careless, hurtful, and deceitful words to others. The Spirit also will give us discernment regarding the deceitful words of others, so that we will not be misled by lies.

Yielding to God means being full of His Word. Study and memorize these prayers from the Bible so that they will be in your heart and help you control your tongue:

> *Set a guard, O Lord, over my mouth; keep watch over the door of my lips* (Psalm 141:3).

> *Let the words of my mouth and the meditation of my heart be acceptable in Your sight, O Lord, my rock and my Redeemer* (Psalm 19:14).

Words of Freedom

The language of faith is the language of freedom. It is the language of encouragement and hope. The language of faith is the language of a child that says not, "I believe, but…" or "I will believe when…" or "I will believe if…" but, "I believe…period." True faith language is the creative, positive language of the Word of God. His Word brings life and freedom:

> *It is the Spirit who gives life; the flesh profits nothing. The words that I speak to you are spirit, and they are life.…But Simon Peter answered Him, "Lord, to whom shall we go? You have the words of eternal life"* (John 6:63, 68 NKJV).

> *Then Jesus said…"If you abide in My word, you are My disciples indeed. And you shall know the truth, and the truth shall make you free"* (John 8:31–32 NKJV).

Because Jesus is the living Word, and because He is the way, the truth, and the life (see John 14:6), His teachings give us life, guidance, and freedom. In the Garden of Gethsemane, Jesus prayed to the Father, *"Not My will, but Yours be done"* (Luke 22:42), and the Father led Him to the cross. On the cross, Jesus' last words were, *"It is finished"*—words that are full of meaning for us. He gave His life that we might go free from the tyranny of sin. He died so that we could live. His death on the cross is a "finished" work! The death and resurrection of Jesus Christ defeated the devil and granted us new power:

> *The Son of God appeared for this purpose, to destroy the works of the devil* (1 John 3:8).

> *For I am not ashamed of the gospel, for it is the power of God for salvation to everyone who believes, to the Jew first and also to the Greek* (Romans 1:16).

> *For God has not given us a spirit of fear, but of power and of love and of a sound mind* (2 Timothy 1:7 NKJV).

> *I have been crucified with Christ; and it is no longer I who live, but Christ lives in me; and the life which I now live in the flesh I live by faith in the Son of God, who loved me and gave Himself up for me* (Galatians 2:20).

If you are born again, Christ lives in you. Therefore, when you speak His words, you overrule the lies of Satan. Jesus' words bring overcoming power to every circumstance of your life.

One characteristic of the language of faith is that it *edifies*. To edify means to lift up, to instruct and improve morally and spiritually. We are to use our tongues to build up rather than to tear down one another. Paul wrote:

> *Let no unwholesome word proceed from your mouth, but only such a word as is good for edification according to the need of the moment, so that it will give grace to those who hear* (Ephesians 4:29).

Harsh, hurtful, biting, and belittling words are never appropriate. Even when we have to say something that others may not want to hear, we can still do it in a spirit of love with kind and compassionate words. Do you remember the song from *Mary Poppins* with the words, "Just a spoonful of sugar helps the medicine go down"? The same is true when we deal with others. God's Word is truly sweet medicine, particularly when used wisely and appropriately in specific situations:

How sweet are Your words to my taste! Yes, sweeter than honey to my mouth! (Psalm 119:103)

Pleasant words are a honeycomb, sweet to the soul and healing to the bones (Proverbs 16:24).

A man has joy in an apt [unusually fitted] *answer, and how delightful is a timely word!* (Proverbs 15:23)

Some situations may not be pleasant or easy, but loving words will always help heal and encourage.

The Power of Praise

Another aspect of the language of faith is that it is the language of praise. Our tongues were created to praise the Lord! God created man for fellowship. From the beginning, we were meant to praise and worship God. God still seeks those who will worship Him in spirit and in truth. Jesus said to the Samaritan woman at the well:

But an hour is coming, and now is, when the true worshipers will worship the Father in spirit and truth; for such people the Father seeks to be His worshipers (John 4:23).

Again and again the psalms tell us to praise the Lord for His mighty works and to magnify His name:

Sing praise to the Lord, you His godly ones, and give thanks to His holy name (Psalm 30:4).

Shout joyfully to God, all the earth; sing the glory of His name; make His praise glorious (Psalm 66:1–2).

Enter His gates with thanksgiving and His courts with praise. Give thanks to Him, bless His name (Psalm 100:4).

Praise the Lord! Oh give thanks to the Lord, for He is good; for His lovingkindness is everlasting (Psalm 106:1).

Praise the Lord! Praise, O servants of the Lord, praise the name of the Lord (Psalm 113:1).

> *Praise the* Lord*! Praise the* Lord*, O my soul! I will praise the* Lord *while I live; I will sing praises to my God while I have my being* (Psalm 146:1–2).

> *Let everything that has breath praise the* Lord*. Praise the* Lord*!* (Psalm 150:6)

"God still seeks those who will worship Him in spirit and in truth."

The book of Psalms is really a collection of sacred songs and poems used in worship. Singing worship songs is one of the most effective ways to praise the Lord. Even though you may not have a beautiful singing voice, your praises are beautiful to His ear. What a wonderful way to use the tongue!

We are to enter into God's presence with praise because it opens the door for God to do powerful things in our lives. There is such power in an atmosphere of group praise that miracles can and do happen. An attitude of praise is a witness to unsaved people. In the early church, many unbelievers were born again because they saw the unity and praise among the believers:

> *Day by day continuing with one mind in the temple, and breaking bread from house to house, they were taking their meals together with gladness and sincerity of heart, praising God and having favor with all the people. And the Lord was adding to their number day by day those who were being saved* (Acts 2:46–47).

There are numerous testimonies in the Bible of miracles happening during times of praise. When Paul and Silas were in the Philippian prison they sang praises to God. Suddenly an earthquake shook the building and their chains fell off—theirs as well as those of the other prisoners. If they escaped, the jailer would pay with his life. Rather than let that happen, the jailer prepared to kill himself. When Paul assured him that no one had escaped, the jailer asked, *"Sirs, what must I do to be saved?"* (Acts 16:30) They answered, *"Believe in the Lord Jesus, and you will be saved, you and your household"* (Acts 16:31). The jailer did believe, along with his entire family. Because of the worship and praise of two strong believers, an entire pagan family came to faith in Christ! Praise is powerful!

Just Ask Daddy

Faith language is also the language of prayer. Through prayer God has given us a way to be free from worry and anxiety. In spite of this, most people, including far too many believers, continue trying to carry their own burdens. Perhaps it is the desire to be "in control" that keeps them from turning to the Lord. When we fail to pray, we rob ourselves of peace, joy, and the faith-building experience of seeing God work in our lives. Paul knew the importance of prayer as well as its rewards:

> *Be anxious for nothing, but in everything by prayer and supplication with thanksgiving let your requests be made known to God. And the peace of God, which surpasses all comprehension, will guard your hearts and your minds in Christ Jesus* (Philippians 4:6–7).

Several years ago, I experienced the truth of this Scripture for myself when three major crises hit at one time. My mother learned that she had a brain tumor, our son was having some problems, and our ministry was going through a tremendous financial struggle. I recognized immediately the spiritual nature of these attacks, that Satan was trying to steal my mother's health, my son, and the finances that would pay our bills.

My first response was to pray. Following Philippians 4:6, I made my requests known to God. Then, turning to the Scriptures, I spoke the Word of God to the afflicted area of my mother's brain and over my son and his situation. The financial matter was the hardest struggle. While ministering at another church, the Lord led me to stand in faith for their budget, even though we were in great need ourselves.

I said "Lord, You want me to believe for their big budget when I'm going through a difficult financial trial myself?" I began to murmur and to speak negative words. I complained about having to work so hard—studying, traveling, and memorizing the Word. In the middle of my complaining, God spoke to me from His Word: *"Your God whom you constantly serve will Himself deliver you"* (Daniel 6:16). After that I had an assurance in my heart, a wonderful peace and confidence in Him.

When the answers to my prayer came, they came quickly! I got a call that my mother had gone to a brain specialist and a new x-ray showed no trace of a tumor—not even a shadow! Next, I got a call that our son had made a dramatic turnaround. Finally, a miraculous financial breakthrough occurred in our ministry!

Don't let your life be eaten up by anxiety. Don't try to be "Super Christian" and handle all your problems alone. Your words can have a powerful effect on your life if you will in faith simply make your requests known to God. Don't make things so difficult on yourself. Go to God like a child to his father. Just ask Daddy!

Prayer is also for the purpose of interceding for the needs of others. As believers we have a holy responsibility and privilege to speak godly words for people and situations in our world, and particularly for the leaders of our nation as well as those of other nations. God's plan includes all nations and we need to lift up the saved and our brothers and sisters in Christ in other lands. Their leaders need wisdom as much as ours do. Faithful intercession brings God's power and activity into play to help bring His will and purpose to pass in the world. It also enhances our peace and spiritual growth. This is what Paul had in mind when he wrote:

> *First of all, then, I urge that entreaties and prayers, petitions and thanksgivings, be made on behalf of all men, for kings and all who are in authority, so that we may lead a tranquil and quiet life in all godliness and dignity* (1 Timothy 2:1–2).

Prayer can transcend physical distance in bringing spiritual and physical relief to people in need. Just as I prayed for my mother across the miles, you can pray for the physical and spiritual needs of others. A ventriloquist trains to perfect the technique of "throwing his voice" in order to create an illusion, but we have at our disposal a supernatural gift: the ability to send the power of the Word of God into situations anywhere in the world.

Jesus demonstrated this ability more than once:

> *And when Jesus entered Capernaum, a centurion came to Him, imploring Him, and saying, "Lord, my servant is lying paralyzed at home, fearfully tormented." Jesus said to him, "I will come and heal him." But the centurion said, "Lord, I am not worthy for You to come under my roof, but just say the word, and my servant will be healed."...Now when Jesus heard this, He marveled and said to those who were following, "Truly I say to you, I have not found such great faith with anyone in Israel."...And Jesus said to the centurion, "Go; it shall be done for you as you have believed." And the servant was healed that very moment* (Matthew 8:5–8, 10, 13).

The centurion recognized that Jesus had the power to "speak the Word" and heal his servant, no matter how far away he was. Jesus honored that faith and sent the Word that heals!

On another occasion Jesus once again demonstrated how the Word is sent to meet a need. A royal official from Capernaum traveled to Cana to ask Jesus to come and heal his son, who was at the point of death. As a test of the man's faith, Jesus took a different approach:

> *Jesus said to him, "Go; your son lives." The man believed the word that Jesus spoke to him and started off. As he was now going down, his slaves met him, saying that his son was living. So he inquired of them the hour when he began to get better. Then they said to him, "Yesterday at the seventh hour the fever left him." So the father knew that it was at that hour in which Jesus said to him, "Your son lives"; and he himself believed and his whole household* (John 4:50–53).

"God's Word is not limited by distance!"

When the Word of God is spoken in faith in one place, miracles can happen at another place because God's Word is not limited by distance! You have the power to speak God's Word into situations next door, across the country, or around the world! Many times, I have been separated from someone who needed prayer and I confessed the Word: *"He sent His word and healed them, and delivered them from their destructions"* (Psalm 107:20).

Use your mouth to launch the Word of God. Send it into broken homes, to sick friends, tired workers, dried-up finances, ungodly relatives—and watch His Word heal the situation. When sickness attacks, you can speak the Word to your own body. God wants you well: *"Beloved, I pray that in all respects you may prosper and be in good health, just as your soul prospers"* (3 John 2).

Prayer is an incredibly powerful and wonderful part of the language of faith, and it is readily available to you. Don't neglect it and don't be afraid to use it!

Action Follows the Word

You can speak the Word of God in faith to restore a right attitude or bring reconciliation into a broken relationship. Send the Word to the problem and let it be a positive force for restoration. For example, let's say you have hard feelings toward someone who has misused you and you want to get even. Instead of seeking vengeance, express your feelings to God, confess your angry and bitter feelings as sin, and speak faith into the situation: "I have the love of God in my heart, and I forgive this person. By God's power, I will forget the way he wronged me and not try to get even." When you can "send" that word, God will work in the situation. As you continue to confess the love of Christ for that person, you will begin to feel love. Your attitude will change and open the way for God to change the other person's attitude as well.

Jesus constantly declared the words He heard the Father speaking, and that is how He overcame the world. As followers of Jesus, we are supposed to imitate Him, and to do that we must talk as He talked and act as He acted.

It is vital that our actions match our words. This means not only hearing or speaking the Word, but also acting on the Word—putting it into practice in our daily lives. If our tongue is harnessed with the power of God's Word, our deeds have to follow! Faith in action is faith that God blesses:

> *But prove yourselves doers of the word, and not merely hearers who delude themselves. For if anyone is a hearer of the word and not a doer, he is like a man who looks at his natural face in a mirror; for once he has looked at himself and gone away, he has immediately forgotten what kind of person he was. But one who looks intently at the perfect law, the law of liberty, and abides by it, not having become a forgetful hearer but an effectual doer, this man will be blessed in what he does* (James 1:22–25).

By learning to speak the language of faith, you truly can change the circumstances of your life as well as impact the lives of others. Don't let your tongue become a tool of the enemy to trap you in negative and destructive habits and thought patterns. Make the connection between your tongue and the Word of God. Do you want to see the windows of heaven open and the blessings of God pour down into your life? Do you long to see God's power working in your situation? Do you have a desire to be a blessing to others? Learn the language of faith. God's Word is the key, faith is the power, and speaking the Word is the way.

STEPS TO A SIMPLER FAITH

1. Read James 1:26 and James 3:1–2 in several versions of the Bible. Meditate on how you can "bridle your own tongue."
2. Give three or four examples of how God's Word can be used as a positive force. Use both biblical and personal examples.
3. Think about five negative ways you may have used your tongue. Using Scripture, write out five prayers that will help you to avoid the same mistake in the future.
4. Find examples of people in the Bible who spoke their faith and received dramatic results. What habits did they have that you can copy and apply in your own life?
5. If we are to be imitators of God, we need to talk like Him. Write out at least three ways you can begin to talk like God—for instance, "God loves the world"; therefore, "I love those around me."

CHAPTER FOUR

Facing Your Giants With Faith

Medical research has shown that the actions of the body are related to the tongue. It is even suggested that the speech nerve center has power over the entire body. For instance, if someone continually says, "I'm going to become weak," the nerves receive that message and say, "Get ready; we've received instructions to become weak." They then transmit that weakness impulse to the muscles and the rest of the body, resulting in weakness. So in other words, you can control your body and manipulate it however you wish according to the words you speak. If you say, "I have no ability to do this job," right away your body will begin to declare the same thing.

It is no wonder then that Jesus emphasized the importance of our words! Once we realize the impact our words have on our natural nervous system, we can begin to understand their impact in the spiritual realm. Truly, what we say and believe will happen. Remember, Jesus said that faith the size of a mustard seed can move a mountain.

Because our words are so important, we need to make sure that what we say is true and right and in accordance with what God says in His Word. We need to *agree* with God in what He says about us. For example, instead of saying, "I know I'm going to be achy and weak tomorrow because I've caught the flu," say, "I am strong because God is my refuge and strength" (see Psalm 46:1). Rather than saying "I'm a failure; I just can't do it!" say, *"I can do all things through Christ who strengthens me"* (Philippians 4:13 NKJV).

Giving such vocal expression to our faith is called *confessing* our faith. *Nelson's Illustrated Bible Dictionary* defines confession as "an admission of sins and the profession of belief in the doctrines of a particular faith."[6] To confess in this sense basically means to agree. There are two basic New Testament words for "confess." The first is *homologeo*, which means "to assent" or "to acknowledge" or "to promise." This is the word used in Matthew 10:32: *"Therefore everyone who confesses Me before men, I will also confess him before My Father who is in heaven,"* and Romans 10:9: *"That if you confess with your mouth Jesus as Lord, and believe in your heart that God raised Him from the dead, you will be saved."*

The second word for "confess" is *exomologeo* which, in addition to "assent" and "acknowledge," also means "to agree fully." It is found in Philippians 2:11: *"Every tongue will confess that Jesus Christ is Lord, to the glory of God the Father,"* and James 5:16: *"Therefore, confess your sins to one another, and pray for one another so that you may be healed. The effective prayer of a righteous man can accomplish much."*

Confessing the Word of God is a powerful faith builder. Faith is not mind over matter or mental manipulation, but simply believing God's eternal, creative Word. The earth we walk on, the air we breathe, the water we drink, and the sun that warms us all were spoken into being by God. He created them all with the spoken word. God maintains the earth with His Word and He keeps us the same way.

As incredible as it may sound, as a believer you have the power of life and death in the words you speak: *"Death and life are in the power of the tongue, and those who love it will eat its fruit"* (Proverbs 18:21). Confessing right words will have a positive effect on every area of your life. Faith-filled words are your key to dynamic, victorious living! I'm not talking about formulas but a mind-set and attitude of confessing the positive and constructive truth of God's Word rather than the negative and destructive lies of the devil. The first will build your faith while the other will tear it down.

Kenneth Copeland talked about the importance of a positive confession in his book, *Prayer: Your Foundation for Success*. He said that we maintain our faith by keeping our confession in line with the Word of God. And since faith is released by our mouth, the importance of speaking the right words—of making the right confession—cannot be emphasized enough.[7]

We often make faith too difficult. Remember the Roman centurion who said to Jesus, *"Lord...speak the word only, and my servant shall be healed"* (Matthew 8:8 KJV). The context of this verse makes it clear that speaking the Word "only" is a confession of great faith. Great faith is simple faith, without all the ifs, ands, buts, or conditions we tend to add. The centurion did not rest on ceremony or tradition. He simply expressed simple, childlike faith when he said, "Lord, speak the word only." The word of the Lord was all that the centurion needed, and it is all we need.

Grasshopper or Giant Killer?

Sometimes the problems, challenges, and obstacles we face in life can seem as formidable as giants while we feel like pygmies next to them. Our attitude will make the difference between whether we overcome our challenges or they overcome us. The faith we express or fail to express will reveal whether we are grasshoppers or giant killers.

"Faith-filled words are your key to dynamic, victorious living!"

Soon after Moses led the Israelites out of Egypt, they arrived at the border of Canaan, the land God had promised to give them. All they had to do was cross the Jordan River and claim the land. Moses sent twelve spies—one from each tribe—to reconnoiter the land and bring back a report. One of the spies was Joshua, Moses' aide and future successor.

After forty days of scouting the land, the spies returned with a glowing report of its fertility and fruitfulness, even bringing with them a huge cluster of grapes as proof. Nevertheless, ten of the spies indicated that there was a problem:

> *Thus they told him, and said, "We went in to the land where you sent us; and it certainly does flow with milk and honey, and this is its fruit. Nevertheless, the people who live in the land are strong, and the cities are fortified and very large...." Then Caleb quieted the people before Moses and said, "We should by all means go up and take possession of it, for we will surely overcome it." But the men who had gone up*

with him said, "We are not able to go up against the people, for they are too strong for us.... The land through which we have gone, in spying it out, is a land that devours its inhabitants; and all the people whom we saw in it are men of great size....and we became like grasshoppers in our own sight, and so we were in their sight" (Numbers 13:27–28, 30–33).

Although this passage does not mention it, Joshua joined Caleb in the minority report encouraging the people to go in and take the land. It was two against ten, and the ten won. Persuaded by the negative report of the ten spies, the people as a whole lost heart and refused to enter the land. As a result of their disobedience and lack of faith, God judged them and sentenced them to wander in the wilderness outside Canaan for forty years until all that rebellious generation died—all except Joshua and Caleb.

The Israelites failed to enter the Promised Land because they saw their "giants" as unbeatable. Under Joshua's leadership, the next generation learned that was not the case. They crossed the Jordan, entered Canaan, and in victory after victory conquered cities and villages and destroyed or displaced the "giants" who were living there.

What made the difference? Faith. The Israelites under Joshua's leadership were prepared to believe the Word of the Lord and that it applied to them. They took to heart the words that Moses shared with them shortly before he died:

All these blessings will come upon you and overtake you if you obey the Lord your God: Blessed shall you be in the city, and...in the country. Blessed shall be [your] *offspring...and the produce of your ground and the offspring of your beasts, the increase of your herd and the young of your flock. Blessed shall be your basket and your kneading bowl. Blessed shall you be when you come in, and blessed shall you be when you go out. The Lord shall cause your enemies who rise up against you to be defeated before you; they will come out against you one way and will flee before you seven ways.... The Lord will make you abound in prosperity...The Lord will open for you His good storehouse, the heavens...The Lord will make you the head and not the tail, and you only will be above, and you will not be underneath, if you*

> *listen to the commandments of the* LORD *your God, which I charge you today, to observe them carefully"* (Deuteronomy 28:2–7, 11–13).

As a child of God, these promises are for you, too. Even though sometimes you may feel like a grasshopper next to the gigantic challenges and obstacles you face, learning to speak and claim the Word of God in faith will bring you victory. Speaking the right confession will cause you to prevail. This means learning who you really are in Christ and claiming your rights and privileges accordingly. You are not a grasshopper; you are a giant killer!

Concerning our confession, Don Gossett wrote:

> Since God cannot lie, we cannot lie when our confession is what God says. For example, we are who God says we are, we have what God says we have, and we can do what God says we can do. We should be confessing who we are, what we have, and what we can do by faith, regardless of whether or not we can see it or feel it. Our confession is our belief of who we are in Christ Jesus.[8]

Speak God's Word to Activate Your Faith

What was the secret of Joshua's great success as a leader? He learned to confess the Word of God and walk in obedience. For many years Joshua had been Moses' right-hand man and was groomed as his successor. One day Moses would die, leaving Joshua to lead the children of Israel into the Promised Land. When that day finally came, the situation looked bleak. With Moses' death, Joshua no longer had someone to lean on. He was on his own, so he had to take the Word of God in his mouth and put it into practice.

Shortly after Moses died, the Lord spoke to Joshua:

> *Be strong and courageous, for you shall give this people possession of the land which I swore to their fathers to give them. Only be strong and very courageous; be careful to do according to all the law which Moses My servant commanded you; do not turn from it to the right or to the left, so that you may have success wherever you go. This book of the law shall not depart from your mouth, but you shall meditate on it day and*

night, so that you may be careful to do according to all that is written in it; for then you will make your way prosperous, and then you will have success (Joshua 1:6–8).

Joshua became successful in every area of his life because he believed what God said in His Word. Joshua flourished in his spiritual life, his family life, his finances, and his life as a leader because he disciplined himself to meditate on the Word. At that time only the first five books of the Bible had been written, but Joshua was faithful with what he had! Can you imagine meditating on and speaking the books of Leviticus and Numbers day and night?

Joshua was over eighty years old when he took charge of the Israelites. What does that say about those of us who feel like we're "over the hill" at fifty, blaming our age for loss of memory and energy? Joshua proved that it doesn't have to be that way. He was exceptionally busy leading a nation of over a million people. He was not only their spiritual and military leader, but also the one responsible for providing them with clothes, water, and food.

"Joshua's secret to success was confessing the Word of God and walking in obedience."

Speaking and meditating on God's Word gave Joshua incredible military success. The walls of Jericho fell because he obeyed the Lord's command. He directed the people to march around the walls once a day for six days, seven times on the seventh day, and then to shout with all their might. The walls fell flat and the Israelites took the city.

During another battle, God sent huge hailstones that battered the enemy, but missed Joshua and his men:

As they fled before Israel, while they were descending [the pass] to Beth-horon, the Lord cast great stones from the heavens on them as far as Azekah, killing them. More died because of the hailstones than the Israelites slew with the sword (Joshua 10:11 AMP).

Can you imagine the hand of a Canaanite on your throat when suddenly he is knocked to the ground by a huge ball of hail? Our miracle-working

God sometimes even commands natural events to protect His children. If we speak the Word of God in faith and walk in obedience, we can be just as victorious in our lives as the Israelites were in Joshua's day.

Certainly, Joshua was a great warrior, but was he prosperous in other areas of his life? Yes, indeed. He was successful in business. When the land of Canaan was taken, Joshua became very wealthy after he received a large mountainous tract of land named Timnath-serah, which means "double portion—city of the sun."

> *When they had finished dividing the land for inheritance by their boundaries, the Israelites gave an inheritance among them to Joshua son of Nun. According to the word of the Lord they gave him the city for which he asked—Timnath-serah in the hills of Ephraim. And he built the city and dwelt in it"* (Joshua 19:49–50 AMP).

Because of Joshua's faithfulness and obedience, God saw to it that he got what he wanted in life. In addition to the wealth of real estate, Joshua was also richly blessed in his family and home life. Toward the end of his long life, Joshua summed up his success by challenging the rest of the people to live as he had lived:

> *Now, therefore, fear the LORD and serve Him in sincerity and truth; and put away the gods which your fathers served beyond the River and in Egypt, and serve the LORD. If it is disagreeable in your sight to serve the LORD, choose for yourselves today whom you will serve: whether the gods which your fathers served which were beyond the River, or the gods of the Amorites in whose land you are living; but as for me and my house, we will serve the LORD* (Joshua 24:14–15).

Joshua made the choice to speak God's Word, and the result was great success. If it worked for Joshua, it will work for you! You have God's Word just like Joshua. Start speaking the Word into every situation and watch your life change. You activate faith with your mouth by saying what God says and agreeing with it. Try it! Your life will never be the same!

Junior Giant Killer

Are you facing a "giant" in your life today—a physical ailment, marital problem, lack of finances, difficulty with your children, or strife at work? Depending on the specific circumstances, any situation can seem overwhelming. Compared to your problems, you may feel as small as a grasshopper, but your feelings are wrong. As a Christian you are in covenant relationship with the God who created the universe. God will fight on your side no matter how big or small you may feel. Like David against Goliath, you can fight your giants with confidence, armed with the Word of God. Don't be deceived into believing that you can't win when problems seem so much bigger than you are. Practice your covenant relationship with God. Shout His promises at your giants and watch them fall!

"Your giant can become your servant."

The Philistines were enemies of Israel and their champion warrior, Goliath, was literally a giant. The Bible says Goliath stood *"six cubits and a span,"* or a little more than nine feet tall! (See 1 Samuel 17:4.) They had gathered their armies to battle the Israelites at a place called Socoh, which means "hedge, enclosure, or shut-in place." Socoh was located in the territory allotted to the tribe of Judah, which means "praise."

When you praise the Lord, your praise builds a hedge around you, shutting you in with God. Think of being shut in with God! You may not feel like rejoicing because of the trial, but you can rejoice because of the victory you will receive!

> *Consider it all joy, my brethren, when you encounter various trials, knowing that the testing of your faith produces endurance. And let endurance have its perfect result, so that you may be perfect and complete, lacking in nothing* (James 1:2–4).

Where does this "joy" come from? It comes from those times of being "shut in" with God: *"The joy of the Lord is your strength and stronghold"* (Nehemiah 8:10 AMP).

The Philistines and the Israelites were gathered on opposite mountaintops, with a large valley between them. Goliath boasted to Israel that if anyone could kill him, the Philistines would be their servants. This realization is vital! Your giant can become your servant! Let God's Word be your weapon and allow the problems in your life to take you to a higher place in God.

For forty days Goliath shouted at the Israelites, mocking God, taunting and ridiculing them, and causing them to fear for their lives. Goliath challenged them to send out a man to fight him, but King Saul and all his men were afraid:

> *Again the Philistine said, "I defy the ranks of Israel this day; give me a man that we may fight together." When Saul and all Israel heard these words of the Philistine, they were dismayed and greatly afraid* (1 Samuel 17:10–11).

The Philistines' continual boasting about how mighty they were convinced the Israelites that they were weak and useless. This is a common tactic of the enemy. He wants you to become so overwhelmed by the giants in your life that you give in to fear and give up without trying.

David provides a wonderful example of how to deal with giants. He was not impressed with the enemy and was not afraid of Goliath. David was impressed with the power of the God of Israel and was ready to do battle in God's strength. Interestingly enough, David was not even a soldier. He was a shepherd, the youngest of his father's sons, and had gone to the scene of battle simply to bring food to his older brothers who were serving in the army. When David first heard Goliath's challenge, he was amazed that anyone would have the nerve to defy God's people:

> *Who is this uncircumcised Philistine, that he should taunt the armies of the living God?* (1 Samuel 17:26)

When Saul heard about David and his question, he brought David to him. David offered to fight Goliath himself:

> *David said to Saul, "Let no man's heart fail on account of him; your servant will go and fight with this Philistine." Then Saul said to David, "You are not able to go against this Philistine to fight with him; for you are but a youth while he has been a warrior from his youth." But David said to Saul, "Your servant was tending his father's sheep...Your servant has killed both the lion and the bear; and this uncircumcised Philistine will be like one of them, since he has taunted the armies of the living God." And David said, "The* Lord *who delivered me from the paw of the lion and from the paw of the bear, He will deliver me from the hand of this Philistine"* (1 Samuel 17:32–34, 36–37).

A Battle Plan for Dealing With Giants

By examining the way David approached his confrontation with Goliath, we can see a six-step battle plan we can use in confronting and defeating our own giants.

Step #1: Assess the situation—understand the battle ahead.

David took one look at the situation and saw the battle for what it was: the devil's army against God's army rather than the Philistines against the Israelites. Because David saw the situation in this light, he knew where the true power lay and that victory did not depend on armed might or military prowess. That is why he had no hesitation in volunteering to fight Goliath man-to-man. David was not reckless; he just understood the battle. In the same way, we need to understand that our battles are not our own. No matter how great the giant we face, the power of the Lord is greater.

Step #2: Trust the *Lord* for victory—not your own strength.

The devil will try to discourage you by playing on your weaknesses. David, however, did a very important thing. He told Saul about his many victories against lions and bears, then made a strong statement of faith: *"The LORD who delivered me from the paw of the lion and from the paw of the bear, He will deliver me from the hand of this Philistine"* (1 Samuel 17:37). Saul tried to give David his armor to wear, but it was too heavy and David could not move around very well, so he took it off. In the end, David went out armed only with his sling and the power of God. What more did he need? In the same way, don't try to fight your giant in your own strength; trust the Lord for victory, and He will fight the giant for you.

Step #3: Speak your faith—let your mouth activate your body.

When problems come your way, remember what the Lord has done for you in the past. Rehearse your victories, and then speak your faith.

David knew that the godly armor of the Word of God would protect him. When Goliath lumbered toward David screaming insults, David calmly replied:

> *You come to me with a sword, a spear, and a javelin, but I come to you in the name of the LORD of hosts, the God of the armies of Israel,*

> *whom you have taunted. This day the LORD will deliver you up into my hands* (1 Samuel 17:45-46).

This was David's way of saying, "You aren't defying me; you're defying the Lord God, and you had better watch out!" David spoke his faith and it activated his body so that he moved confidently to join battle with Goliath. When facing your giant, make sure you infuse your spirit with the Word of God. Speak the Word in faith and it will strengthen you to take the action you need to take.

Step #4: Know the Word of God—don't go into battle without an arsenal.

Before running to meet Goliath, David loaded his bag with five smooth stones for his sling. Never try to fight a giant without weapons. You cannot speak the Word of God unless you *know* the Word of God. The Spirit cannot bring the Word to your remembrance if you don't have it in your mind in the first place. Take time now to begin learning and memorizing God's Word. Learn to put on the armor of God as Paul described in Ephesians 6:10–18. As you do these things, you will find yourself more and more well-equipped for any battle that comes your way.

Step #5: Plan for the unexpected—don't underestimate the enemy.

Just as David collected five smooth stones for ammunition, you need to have more than one Scripture in your arsenal. David wasn't afraid that he would miss Goliath with the first stone; he just wanted to be prepared for the unexpected. Satan may try to toss unexpected things at you, trying to add to your problems. He may come at you from different angles, so you need different "stones" of the Word to hurl at him in order to win the victory. Be prepared, but don't underestimate the enemy.

The Bible account says that David brought Goliath down with a single stone to his forehead. How is this possible? Goliath was not an ordinary, run-of-the-mill enemy. He was enormous and wore massive armor. A heavy bronze helmet covered his head, so how could David kill him? This was a great part of the miracle. The one stone David threw must have penetrated the helmet covering the giant's forehead, although ordinarily a stone would bounce off metal. David's confession of faith made that stone pierce through the bronze, the flesh, and the bone.

The stone sank into the giant's forehead and he fell over. David didn't have a sword, so he ran to the giant, and using Goliath's own sword, cut off his head! Remember, it's not good enough to knock out a problem—you must cut off the problem at its source so it will not return to attack you again!

Step #6: Give God the glory for victory!

How astonished the Philistines were when they saw their champion defeated! Chased by the Israelites, they ran in despair to a place called Ekron, which means "eradication." When you "throw" the Word like a stone, you eradicate—get rid of and wipe out—the enemy's ability to harm you. What David did next shows that he was a very wise young man. Instead of basking in the glory of his victory, he took Goliath's head back to Jerusalem, the city of peace, where God was worshiped. He wanted to be sure that God received all the glory and praise for this great victory. In the same manner, when God enables you to bring down your giant, remember to give Him the praise, honor, and glory for the victory. Be sure to tell others about it as well, so that their faith can be strengthened by the news of God's power to deliver.

Facing Down the Giant of Temptation

One giant we all face is the giant of temptation. Because we live in a fallen, sinful world and because we all have a sin nature that battles against the nature of Christ in us, temptation is a fact of life. Although the Lord never promises to shield us from temptation, He does promise to give us the means of escape: *"No temptation has overtaken you but such as is common to man; and God is faithful, who will not allow you to be tempted beyond what you are able, but with the temptation will provide the way of escape also, so that you will be able to endure it"* (1 Corinthians 10:13).

What is the best way to deal with temptation? As with everything else, turn to the Word of God. In this, our best example is Jesus Himself. Jesus used the Word many times during His ministry on earth, but especially when He was tempted by Satan. At the beginning of His public ministry Jesus spent forty days fasting in the wilderness, where Satan tempted Him:

> *And the tempter came and said to Him, "If You are the Son of God, command that these stones become bread." But He answered and said, "It is written, 'Man shall not live on bread alone, but on every word that proceeds out of the mouth of God.' " Then the devil took Him into the holy city and had Him stand on the pinnacle of the temple, and said to Him, "If You are the Son of God, throw Yourself down; for it is written, 'He will command His angels concerning You,' and 'On their hands they will bear You up, so that You will not strike Your foot against a stone.' " Jesus said to him, "On the other hand, it is written, 'You shall not put the Lord your God to the test' "* (Matthew 4:3–7).

Three times the devil tried to get Jesus to turn away from the path chosen by His Father. On his second attempt, the devil even tried to trick Jesus by quoting a Scripture himself. Three times Jesus countered the temptation with the Scriptures, saying, *"It is written…"*

Satan's third attempt involved a temptation that is still a strong allurement for people today:

> *Again, the devil took Him to a very high mountain and showed Him all the kingdoms of the world and their glory; and he said to Him, "All these things I will give You, if You fall down and worship me"* (Matthew 4:8–9).

Satan is a tricky, devious enemy who will use any tactic to defeat us. How many people in our world today have bowed before Satan because of his promise of worldly wealth and power!

At this point, Jesus grew weary of Satan's games and took a strong stand against him:

> *Go, Satan! For it is written, "You shall worship the Lord your God, and serve Him only"* (Matthew 4:10).

During times of temptation, you should do exactly the same thing Jesus did. Speak the Word of God in faith and you will escape. The devil will have to flee. God will honor His Word and give you deliverance. Once again, of course, you have to *know* the Word of God in order for it to do you any good in facing temptation. That is why it is so important to get into the Word every day.

When Satan says to you, "If you will only...," respond to him with, "It is written...!" Use the power of the Word of God. No matter how great or strong the giant of temptation appears to be, even one Word of God spoken in faith will fell him.

The Prayer of a Giant Killer

Another essential part of dealing with the giants in your life is learning to pray more powerful and faith-filled prayers. By praying according to the will of the Father and by speaking His Word into your situation, you can be delivered from evil and learn how to forgive others. When you pray the Word specifically for your own needs, you will receive powerful answers.

Praying the words "Your will be done" is not a cop-out phrase or an excuse for not taking charge of things. When you pray for God's will—and really mean it—you're going to get God's very best. Your faith is turned loose! You can be assured that He will hear you:

> *This is the confidence which we have before Him, that, if we ask anything according to His will, He hears us. And if we know that He hears us in whatever we ask, we know that we have the requests which we have asked from Him* (1 John 5:14–15).

Undoubtedly you are familiar with the "Lord's Prayer," but do you realize it can be an expression of your faith for a supernatural blessing?

> *Pray, therefore like this: Our Father Who is in heaven, hallowed (kept holy) be Your name. Your kingdom come, Your will be done on earth as it is in heaven. Give us this day our daily bread. And forgive us our debts, as we also have forgiven (left, remitted, and let go of the debts, and have given up resentment against) our debtors. And lead (bring) us not into temptation, but deliver us from the evil one. For Yours is the kingdom and the power and the glory forever. Amen* (Matthew 6:9–13 AMP).

The Lord's Prayer can be divided into six parts: three petitions have to do with God and His glory, and three have to do with our own needs. It is the perfect Bible lesson on speaking your faith. When you pray *"our Father,"* you not only petition the God of the universe, but also your personal Father God. There is awesome power in the name, *Father*, but there is also a close loving relationship because we are God's family—His sons and daughters. He loves us dearly!

"Hallowed be Your name," "Your kingdom come," and *"Your will be done on earth as it is in heaven"* acknowledge our Father God as absolute Lord and Sovereign of the earth. These phrases focus our attention on His holiness and help us express our desire for His will to be done above all.

The kingdom of God transcends time, which means it isn't limited by seasons. God is able and willing to do the same miraculous things today as He has done in the past. When we pray for God to *"give us this day our daily bread,"* we show the Lord that we trust Him to meet our present personal needs.

"Forgive us our debts, as we also have forgiven our debtors" indicates that our Father is able to forgive our sins and help us forgive those who have wronged us. *"Lead us not into temptation, but deliver us from the evil one"* provides our protection from the schemes of Satan to steal from, kill, or destroy us. *Temptation*, as used here, means "testing," which comes from the devil. Although "tests" can be unpleasant, they can be the keys to our success in life. God has already made provision for all your needs, so your confession of faith is based on the truth of the Word.

The beauty of the Lord's Prayer is its simplicity. Less than a hundred words long, it nevertheless expresses everything we need in life. How many times have we heard prayers that went on and on yet never really said anything! How many times have we prayed prayers like that ourselves? A simple prayer is a childlike prayer. Children pray simple prayers, but often they are very beautiful, not only because of their simplicity, but also because of the simple, unquestioning trust with which they are prayed. Prayers do not have to be long or involved to be powerful. All they require is faith. Learn to pray simple prayers with simple faith.

Abiding: The Key to Successful Giant Killing

Our ability to release our faith and deal with the giants in our lives depends ultimately upon our ability to allow the life of Jesus to flow through us. He is the vine; we are the branches. He gives life to the branches and is our total support system. Jesus said:

> *I am the true vine, and My Father is the vinedresser....Abide in Me, and I in you. As the branch cannot bear fruit of itself unless it abides in the vine, so neither can you unless you abide in Me. I am the vine,*

> *you are the branches; he who abides in Me and I in him, he bears much fruit, for apart from Me you can do nothing....If you abide in Me, and My words abide in you, ask whatever you wish, and it will be done for you* (John 15:1, 4–5, 7).

Abiding in Christ means having sustained and continual communion with Him through prayer and His Word. The only way to develop this communion is with patient, daily attention. If God's Word constantly abides in you, you will be instantly ready to confess it: *"For out of the abundance (overflow) of the heart his mouth speaks"* (Luke 6:45 AMP). The more time you spend in prayer and God's Word, the more you will learn to abide in Christ. The more you abide in Christ, the stronger (yet simpler) your faith will become, and the better equipped you will be to face the giants in your life.

God's Word shows you how to ask Him wisely for the things you need. As you ask in God's will, guided by the Holy Spirit and using the Word, He will grant your request. As you *"abide"* in Him, the Holy Spirit will prompt you to ask for the right things. God's Word will teach you how to have continual communion with Him. The more you abide in Christ, the more you will begin to see your giants come tumbling down.

STEPS TO A SIMPLER FAITH

1. Keep a journal of the times God has proven Himself faithful to you. Rehearse your victories and have them available for when the enemy next attacks.
2. Look for opportunities to speak God's Word to bless others.
3. List three things you are believing for and put a Bible verse with each one that demonstrates "confessing" the Word. Speak your confessions daily until you have the answers.
4. Read the Lord's Prayer in several different versions of the Bible. Meditate on how God meets *your* needs.
5. Study John 15:1–16 and write out a personal plan for "abiding" in Him.

CHAPTER FIVE

Fear—Faith's Mortal Enemy

"Daddy, catch me!" The little girl is standing on a chair with her arms wide apart. As her father opens his arms toward her, she leaps into them laughing and squealing with delight. They tumble to the floor, wrestling and playing amidst more squeals and laughter.

Oh, the simple, trusting faith of a child! A little girl jumps into her daddy's arms with no fear, no thought at all that her daddy might *not* catch her. Her trust is absolute. Hers is total, complete, *simple* faith—faith with *no fear*.

We live in a fearful world and as we grow older, fear often replaces the simple trust we knew as children. Fear can be a healthy thing, particularly as it helps us flee danger or escape a hazardous situation. *Living* in fear, however, is *not* healthy. God never intended for us to live fear-filled lives. Adam and Eve knew no fear in the Garden of Eden. Fear followed on the heels of sin. Ever since the fall in the Garden, human life has been an ongoing battle against fear.

The Bible says that Jesus came to *"destroy the works of the devil"* (1 John 3:8). One of those "works" He came to destroy is fear. Many times Jesus said, "Do not fear," or "Be not afraid." Just as the little girl above implicitly trusted her father without fear, fear should not be a characteristic quality for us as children of our heavenly Father. In one of his letters to

Timothy, his young protégé, Paul wrote, *"For God has not given us a spirit of fear, but of power and of love and of a sound mind"* (2 Timothy 1:7 NKJV). Fear is the mortal enemy of faith.

In many ways, fear and faith are opposites. We use the word *faith* to express belief for something good, and the word *fear* to express belief in something bad. While fear makes faith fruitless, faith also can cancel out fear. Fear is perhaps our greatest foe. It is certainly Satan's most powerful and reliable weapon against us. God does not want us to live in fear, and He has equipped us to deal with it. Through His Spirit we have the wisdom to discern our enemy as well as the weapon with which to fight him and win!

"Faith submits and resists; fear cuts and runs."

Fear and faith both are motivators; they spur us to act, but in different ways. Faith leads us to step out and act in the way God instructs in His Word. Fear, on the other hand, will cause us to move in the opposite direction. It will drive us to run away and try to avoid the battle. It also allows the devil to chase us and beat up on us. As believers, we are not supposed to give in to Satan. James 4:7 says, *"Submit therefore to God. Resist the devil and he will flee from you."* Faith submits and resists; fear cuts and runs.

There is a clear relationship between fear and faith: Both originate from information we receive. Faith is built on information from God and His Word. Fear is based on negative information that comes from many different sources: neighbors, doctors, newspapers, weather reports, news reports, etc. The devil takes these negative items in the natural world and stirs them up in our minds until we become fearful of everything around us. Fear arises from believing bad news without a sense of hope. In this sense, then, fear is actually faith in something we don't want to happen.

Understand Your Enemy

The basic New Testament word for "fear" is the Greek word *phobos*, which means fear caused by the intimidation of an enemy, or to be in dread or terror. A "phobia" is considered to be an irrational fear—a fear that is based on an unrealistic expectation of something that *might* happen. What terrifies you? What intimidates you? What do you dread? Are you *agoraphobic*—fearful of crowds or public places? Are you *acrophobic*—afraid of heights? Are you *claustrophobic*—afraid of enclosed spaces?

Perhaps your fears are not easily identified. Simple insecurity—a lack of confidence in yourself—can be a by-product of fear: "What if I try, but fail? What will people think of me? I'm afraid I'm not good enough." Many times I have awakened in the night and started to worry. Then I catch myself and bring to mind Proverbs 16:3: *"Commit your works to the LORD and your plans will be established."* The devil likes to harass us through our thought-life. If he can get to us through our minds, he can control our lives. If we commit our works to the Lord, however, our thought-life will come into line, Satan will have no access to our minds, and fear will find no foothold to overwhelm us.

All of us have negative thoughts at one time or another, but we can learn to take control of such thoughts. God has given us not a *"spirit of fear"* but *"a sound mind"*! When we put faith in the place of fear, fear disappears. We can become *aphobos*—"without fear." Consider praying Luke 1:74: *"Grant us that we, being delivered from the hand of our enemies, might serve Him without fear [aphobos]"* (NKJV).

Other root words for "fear" include *deilia*, which means "cowardice and timidity," and *pachad*, "to be on guard, having a fear of death." Several Bible versions use the word *timidity* instead of *fear* in 2 Timothy 1:7. God's Word neutralizes *pachad* or fear of death: "[He will] *free those who through fear of death were subject to slavery all their lives"* (Hebrews 2:15). God has given us the power to overcome the fears that attack us.

Satan desires to keep us bound by fear all our lives because if fear rules our lives, we cannot act in faith. We will be exiles in enemy territory, afraid to claim our inheritance, afraid to use our supernatural weapons, and afraid to declare whom we serve. We need to remember that it is the Spirit of God in us who overcomes the enemy: *"You are from God, little children, and have overcome them; because greater is He who is in you than he who is in the world"* (1 John 4:4).

There is another kind of fear that the Bible talks about, a positive fear: the fear of God. In Greek it is the word *eulabeia*, which means, "caution and reverence; godly, holy and reverent fear." This is not a negative fear, but the fear of awe and reverence toward God in His majesty and glory. There is a beautiful worship song that includes the phrase, "Mighty God, to whom all praise is due, I stand in awe of You." That is what it means to "fear" God: to stand in awe of Him, not in terror or dread, but in reverence and praise, confident of our relationship with Him as His children, but properly respectful of His deity.

One example of the use of *eulabeia* is Hebrews 12:28: *"Therefore, since we are receiving a kingdom which cannot be shaken, let us have grace, by which we may serve God acceptably with reverence and godly fear [eulabeia]"* (NKJV). Fear of God is godly, holy fear of wonder and reverence, and if we are to have a right relationship with our loving Father, we will have this type of "fear" of Him. We willingly choose to exercise *eulabeia*, the God-given, healthy fear of the Lord.

"Do Not Fear!"

Depending on which one you feed, either faith or fear will grow a crop in your life. Faith will yield a harvest of God's best for you, while fear will bring you only the devil's worst. Job 3:25 says, *"For what I fear comes upon me, and what I dread befalls me."* Throughout His Word, the Lord continually encourages us with the words, "Do not fear!" Fear will only produce the very thing we don't want.

"Fear will produce the very thing we don't want."

Most of our fears we pick up as children and carry throughout life. Parents often transfer their own fears to their children through words, actions, and attitudes. Even offhand remarks by an adult can mark a child forever. Generational curses of fear, if not broken, can immobilize us later in life.

What do you fear more than anything else? Losing your job? Losing a child? Losing your spouse? Losing your health? Losing your mind? Whatever the source of your fear, ultimately it is a tool of the devil to keep you in bondage and drive out your faith in God. Satan uses bad news, well-meaning friends, and adverse circumstances to sow doubt and fear in your mind. As long as you continue to dwell on negative things, the enemy will prevent you from taking your "promised land."

Don't forget what happened to the Israelites after they came out of Egypt. God freed them from slavery and was ready to lead them into the Promised Land of Canaan. Heeding the dismal report given by ten of the spies Moses had sent into the land, however, the people as a whole allowed fear to rob them of their promise. Rather than trust in God's promise and power, they succumbed to fear of their own weakness and the apparent strength of the enemy. They let Satan destroy their self-image. Compared to the giants, they saw themselves as little grasshoppers. In their own eyes, they became losers instead of winners. All those who allowed fear to destroy their faith wandered in the wilderness until they died. They never entered into their promise.

If you give in to fear, it will become your master and hold you in slavery to things from which God wants to set you free. Fear that they won't receive healing keeps some people sick. On the other hand, in a twisted way, some people don't really want to be healed because they fear they will not be able to handle new responsibilities. No matter where it comes from, fear is a crippling, cruel, unrelenting, and unforgiving taskmaster!

Instead of giving in to fear, we should take heed of God's words to Joshua when it was time to take the children of Israel into Canaan:

> *Have I not commanded you? Be strong and of good courage; do not be afraid, nor be dismayed, for the LORD your God is with you wherever you go* (Joshua 1:9 NKJV).

This time the people were ready. Taking God at His Word and faithfully following Joshua's leadership, the Israelites took Canaan. They made the Promised Land their own.

Be Anxious for Nothing

The Word of God is always our best weapon against fear.

When our son Michael was 16 or 17, he wanted to buy a car. After a little searching he found one that he liked and the seller, a pastor, let him bring it home to try it out. Early the next morning when I went to wake Michael, he was not in his room. Seeing his window open, I began to feel very uneasy.

I ran to the front of the house, looked out the window, and saw that the car was missing. Instantly my heart filled with fear. *Oh dear God*, I thought, *where is my son*? Wild thoughts started running through my mind as fear almost overwhelmed me. *Lord, he has that pastor's car, and he doesn't even have a driver's license. If he gets caught driving—it could really be serious!*

You know what that kind of fear is like—your heart begins to pound and your breath gets shallow. Finally I turned to the Lord, "God, I don't want to be overwhelmed by fear—fill me with faith! Please, quickly give me a Scripture." The Lord reminded me of Haggai 2:5: *"As for the promise which I made you when you came out of Egypt, My Spirit is abiding in your midst; do not fear!"*

I could almost hear the Lord saying, "Marilyn, I brought you out of the world and I have a covenant with you. You belong to Me, so don't be afraid. My Spirit is with you and I'll take care of this." All day long we wondered where Michael was, and all day long I quoted that Scripture to keep my fear at bay. Although I did not know Michael's whereabouts, I was at peace that the Lord knew and was in control.

Michael was to be at work at five o'clock that afternoon, and when we called his place of employment, he was there! He and the car were both safe. Because I had fought fear with the Word of God, I had peace even before I knew for certain that Michael was all right.

Worry is a by-product of fear. A fearful person is worried, anxious, and constantly wondering what terrible event will happen next. It is extremely hard to trust God when we are worrying because anxiety is a hindrance to our faith. On that day when I did not know where Michael was, I could easily have been overcome with worry had I not given everything over to the Lord and spoken His Word in faith over the situation. When we walk by faith, we will not be saddled with worry. Faith defuses worry by giving it to Jesus.

God's Word makes it clear that we are to trust Him and not give in to fear or worry. The rewards of faith are great:

> *Be anxious for nothing, but in everything by prayer and supplication with thanksgiving let your requests be made known to God. And the peace of God, which surpasses all comprehension, will guard your hearts and your minds in Christ Jesus* (Philippians 4:6–7).

> *Therefore humble yourselves [demote, lower yourselves in your own estimation] under the mighty hand of God, that in due time He may exalt you. Casting the whole of your care [all your anxieties, all your worries,*

all your concerns, once and for all] on Him, for He cares for you affectionately, and cares about you watchfully (1 Peter 5:6–7 AMP).

Consequences of Fear

Just as faith brings great rewards, fear steals rewards and can result in serious consequences. For one thing, fear can keep someone from being healed:

> *And they brought to Him a paralytic lying on a bed. Seeing their faith, Jesus said to the paralytic, "Take courage, son; your sins are forgiven." And some of the scribes said to themselves, "This fellow blasphemes." And Jesus knowing their thoughts said, "Why are you thinking evil in your hearts? Which is easier, to say, 'Your sins are forgiven,' or to say, 'Get up, and walk'? But so that you may know that the Son of Man has authority on earth to forgive sins"—then He said to the paralytic, "Get up, pick up your bed and go home." And he got up and went home* (Matthew 9:2–7).

Although the paralyzed man in this passage was healed, he could easily not have been. His fear could have kept him from coming to Jesus for the help he needed. Obviously, his main problem was sin. Jesus said, "*Take courage, son; your sins are forgiven.*" Perhaps this means that the man was fearful because of his sins and may have come close to not seeking Jesus at all. Once he did, however, and had his sins forgiven, the way was opened for him to be healed.

Don't let fear—particularly fear over your sin—keep you or your loved ones from seeking the Lord's help. Take courage; Jesus is interceding for you right now, and if you come to Him, He will never turn you away:

> *For there is one God, and one mediator also between God and men, the man Christ Jesus* (1 Timothy 2:5).

> *Christ Jesus is He who died, yes, rather who was raised, who is at the right hand of God, who also intercedes for us* (Romans 8:34).

> *All that the Father gives Me will come to Me, and the one who comes to Me I will certainly not cast out* (John 6:37).

The woman who was healed of a twelve-year hemorrhage by touching the hem of Jesus' cloak is another example of a person overcoming fear in order to receive healing. This woman could easily have let fear and shame over her condition keep her from going out in public for help. Fear of the law could have bound her also, since her uncleanness made it unlawful for her to mingle in crowds. Nevertheless, she laid aside her fears and pressed forward to Jesus, who said to her, *"Daughter, take courage; your faith has made you well"* (Matthew 9:22).

Both the paralytic and the woman with the hemorrhage had to overcome fear and move in faith. By acting in faith, however small it may have been, they released the power of the Word of God and received their healing.

Illness can produce fear just as fear can produce illness. Don't let fear keep you or a loved one from taking an illness to Jesus. Stay in control and keep yourself focused on God's promises. Otherwise your mind will become Satan's playground, and he will try to torment you with irrational and unfounded thoughts. There is no need for fear because Jesus is aware of your helplessness, and He has already dealt with every physical ailment: *"He sent His word and healed them, and delivered them from their destructions"* (Psalm 107:20).

Here are some guidelines for dealing with fear and pressing forward in faith for healing:

- Act on your faith and not on your fear (2 Timothy 1:7).
- Confess your sins, including your fears, to God (James 5:16).
- Tell your mountain (illness) to depart (Mark 11:22–23).
- Have the elders of the church anoint you with oil (James 5:14–15).
- Pray the prayer of faith (John 15:7).
- Speak the Word of life over your body daily (Proverbs 4:20–22).

There is a greater consequence to fear than simply missing a healing. Fear and unbelief head the list of sins that lead to eternal death. Those who are afraid to trust Jesus in this life will have to be without Him for eternity:

> *But for the cowardly* [fearful] *and unbelieving and abominable and murderers and immoral persons and sorcerers and idolaters and all*

> *liars, their part will be in the lake that burns with fire and brimstone, which is the second death* (Revelation 21:8).

Don't let fear run and ruin your life! Feed faith by claiming and speaking God's Word into your circumstances.

Courage or Cowardice?

Another common source of fear is the feeling of being threatened by our surroundings or by other people. Common sense tells us to avoid dark alleys or other unsafe situations, but sometimes we end up in danger through no fault of our own. If that happens to you, what will you do? How will you handle it? Depending on the specific situation and your personality, fear can either put wings on your feet and help you flee, or paralyze you and root you to the spot.

Physical danger is not the only thing that can cause you to feel threatened. Your coworkers could say things about you behind your back leaving you fearful for your reputation or even of losing your job. Perhaps some folks at your church have it in for you for some reason. In some cases, your fears may even be well-founded. Rather than trying to fight and defend yourself in the natural, learn to turn your conflict over to God:

> *The fear of man brings a snare, but he who trusts in the* Lord *will be exalted* (Proverbs 29:25).

> *Finally, be strong in the Lord and in the strength of His might. Put on the full armor of God, so that you will be able to stand firm against the schemes of the devil. For our struggle is not against flesh and blood, but against the rulers, against the powers, against the world forces of this darkness, against the spiritual forces of wickedness in the heavenly places. Therefore, take up the full armor of God, so that you will be able to resist in the evil day, and having done everything, to stand firm* (Ephesians 6:10–13).

When the apostle Paul stood to speak before the Sanhedrin in Jerusalem, he could have been afraid because his life was in danger:

> *And as a great dissension was developing, the commander was afraid Paul would be torn to pieces by them and ordered the troops to go down*

> *and take him away from them by force, and bring him into the barracks. But on the night immediately following, the Lord stood at his side and said, "Take courage; for as you have solemnly witnessed to My cause at Jerusalem, so you must witness at Rome also"* (Acts 23:10–11).

The Sanhedrin opposed Paul because of his strong and courageous stance as a follower of Christ. Although he faced danger, persecution, and hardship for the sake of the Gospel everywhere he turned, Paul refused to run away. His faith gave him boldness and banished his fear. The Lord had told him he would preach the Gospel in Rome, and he believed it without question. Paul knew that nothing would happen to him before the Lord's promise was fulfilled. The book of Acts ends with Paul in Rome, under house arrest, but preaching and teaching the Gospel freely for two years.

> "Learn to turn your conflict over to God."

Paul was not a child, but he had a childlike faith, and that faith gave him boldness. Long ago he had learned to take God at His word without question. He knew that he had immediate and continual access to his Father, and that made all the difference. Once we learn to trust God as simply and completely as Paul did, we can be as bold in the Lord as he was. Simple faith cancels out fear:

> *When I am afraid, I will put my trust in You. In God, whose word I praise, in God I have put my trust; I shall not be afraid. What can mere man do to me?* (Psalm 56:3–4)

> *God is love, and the one who abides in love abides in God, and God abides in him....There is no fear in love; but perfect love casts out fear, because fear involves punishment, and the one who fears is not perfected in love. We love, because He first loved us* (1 John 4:16, 18–19).

> *Let us therefore come boldly to the throne of grace, that we may obtain mercy and find grace to help in time of need* (Hebrews 4:16 NKJV).

Walking on Water

Jesus' disciples slowly began to realize that dealing with fear was going to be an important part of their lives as His followers. The more time they spent with Him, the more evident it became that He would not always be with them and that it might not be either popular or safe to identify with Him. Persecution, although not an appealing thought, was a frightening possibility. Indeed, as they soon discovered, it was a certainty. Jesus tried to help them prepare for what lay ahead and remember that they would not be alone:

> *These things I have spoken to you, so that in Me you may have peace. In the world you have tribulation, but take courage; I have overcome the world* (John 16:33).

Although few of us in this country today have experienced it, persecution remains a real possibility for every believer. In addition, there are many other factors in our world that can be sources of fear if we let them. Even when we are walking in the perfect will of God, fearful circumstances occur because this earth is still in the possession of the enemy. Natural conditions such as blizzards, tornadoes, or earthquakes can give us a feeling of total helplessness, but knowing we can call on God to save us should be a great comfort.

One day, immediately after feeding five thousand people with three loaves of bread and two fish, Jesus sent His disciples across the Sea of Galilee in a boat while He dismissed the crowds. As night fell, a storm arose and the boat was badly battered by the high waves. Simon Peter and the other disciples were battling the winds, rowing in the dark, and probably scared half to death. Nevertheless, they were right where Jesus had sent them. They may not have known it at the time, but Jesus had not left them alone:

> *And in the fourth watch of the night He came to them, walking on the sea. When the disciples saw Him walking on the sea, they were terrified, and said, "It is a ghost!" And they cried out in fear. But immediately Jesus spoke to them, saying, "Take courage, it is I; do not be afraid"* (Matthew 14:25–27).

Recognizing their fear, Jesus immediately calmed them with the words, "*Take courage, it is I; do not be afraid.*" No matter how alone we may feel or how frightening a situation may be that we find ourselves in, we can take courage in the fact that Jesus is always with us; we are never alone:

For He Himself has said, "I will never leave you nor forsake you" (Hebrews 13:5 NKJV).

I will not leave you as orphans; I will come to you (John 14:18).

(The King James Version for this verse says, *"I will not leave you* ***comfortless."***)

I am with you always, even to the end of the age (Matthew 28:20).

Peace I leave with you; My peace I give to you; not as the world gives do I give to you. Do not let your heart be troubled, nor let it be fearful (John 14:27).

When we are willing to trust Jesus no matter what the circumstances, He can enable us to do anything. Fear, however, can cause us to fail. Peter discovered this after he saw Jesus walking on the water:

Peter said to Him, "Lord, if it is You, command me to come to You on the water." And He said, "Come!" And Peter got out of the boat, and walked on the water and came toward Jesus. But seeing the wind, he became frightened, and beginning to sink, he cried out, "Lord, save me!" Immediately Jesus stretched out His hand and took hold of him, and said to him, "You of little faith, why did you doubt?" (Matthew 14:28–31)

Peter was doing fine walking on the water until he looked around and focused on his circumstances. As soon as he took his eyes off Jesus, doubt and then fear overcame him. His physical senses took over: He heard the howling of the wind, saw the storm clouds moving, and felt the thrust of the waves against his body. This change of focus caused Peter to lose sight of his goal. He began to sink, even though moments before he had been walking on the water. In fear and desperation, Peter called out to Jesus, who reached out and saved him.

Jesus also rebuked him: *"You of little faith, why did you doubt?"* Apparently, Peter's faith was not the problem; after all, he had walked on the water for a few seconds. It was when fear took over and his courage failed that Peter began to sink. It only takes a little faith—childlike faith—to walk on water, but it also only takes a little fear to sink us.

Courage Restored

Later on, Simon Peter had another crisis of courage that could have been disastrous for him and for the church as a whole. On the very evening that He was arrested, Jesus spoke these words to Peter:

> *"Simon, Simon, behold, Satan has demanded permission to sift you like wheat; but I have prayed for you, that your faith may not fail; and you, when once you have turned again, strengthen your brothers." But he said to Him, "Lord, with You I am ready to go both to prison and to death!" And He said, "I say to you, Peter, the rooster will not crow today until you have denied three times that you know Me"* (Luke 22:31–34).

Jesus prayed that Simon Peter's faith would not fail—and it didn't. *Wait a minute!* you may be thinking. *Didn't Peter's faith fail when he denied Jesus?* No. Peter certainly did deny Jesus three times, just as Jesus said he would, but it was not Peter's faith that failed; it was his *courage*. Peter loved Jesus with all his heart and knew that He was the Son of God and the Savior of the world. After all, it was Peter who answered Jesus' question, *"Who do you say that I am?"* with the words, *"You are the Christ, the Son of the living God"* (Matthew 16:15–16). Jesus knew all about Peter's faith and understood Peter's struggle with fear, just as He understands ours.

Peter was devastated by the failure of his courage and his inability to stand by his Master's side when the chips were down. After the crucifixion, Peter became depressed and discouraged. One day he decided to go fishing and convinced several of the other disciples to go with him. They fished all night and caught nothing. When morning came, a man on the shore called out to them and asked, *"Children, you do not have any fish, do you?"* then told them exactly where to cast their net. Peter and the others complied, and suddenly they found their net so full of fish that they could not haul it in. It was at this moment that John recognized the man on shore as Jesus:

> *Therefore that disciple whom Jesus loved said to Peter, "It is the Lord." So when Simon Peter heard that it was the Lord, he put his outer garment on (for he was stripped for work), and threw himself into the sea"* (John 21:7).

No effort to walk on water this time; no excuses or bravado; impulsive Peter simply jumped into the water and began to swim to shore because it was the fastest way to get to Jesus. Such was Peter's love for the Lord, even in spite of his own failures.

Jesus had built a fire on the shore and invited the men to bring their fish and eat with Him. After breakfast, He spoke to Peter. He wanted to be sure Peter heard Him, so He called him Simon, which means, "the listening one":

> *So when they had finished breakfast, Jesus said to Simon Peter, "Simon, son of John, do you love Me more than these?" He said to Him, "Yes, Lord; You know that I love You." He said to him, "Tend My lambs." He said to him again a second time, "Simon, son of John, do you love Me?" He said to Him, "Yes, Lord; You know that I love You." He said to him, "Shepherd My sheep." He said to him the third time, "Simon, son of John, do you love Me?" Peter was grieved because He said to him the third time, "Do you love Me?" And he said to Him, "Lord, You know all things; You know that I love You." Jesus said to him, "Tend My sheep"* (John 21:15–17).

Three times Jesus asked Peter if he loved Him, and three times Peter replied that he did. The first two times that Jesus asked, "Do you love Me?" He used the word *agape*, which means, as the Amplified Bible states it, *"reasoning, intentional, spiritual devotion, as one loves the Father."* Both times, when Peter answered, "You know that I love You," he used a different word for "love": *phileo*. This word means *"deep, instinctive, personal affection...as for a close friend"* (John 21:15 AMP). Peter did not feel he could claim the higher kind of love represented by *agape*.

When Jesus asked, "Do you love Me?" for the third time, He used Peter's word, *phileo*. Jesus came down to Peter's level to bring Peter up to His. What was the significance of this? Three times Peter had denied Jesus and now Jesus gave Peter three chances to reaffirm his love for Him. In this way, Peter once again declared the deep love and devotion he held for his Lord.

During this same encounter, Jesus, in His loving way, let Peter know that when his time to die came, he would be able to resist fear:

> *"Truly, truly, I say to you, when you were younger, you used to gird yourself and walk wherever you wished; but when you grow old, you*

> *will stretch out your hands and someone else will gird you, and bring you where you do not wish to go." Now this He said, signifying by what kind of death he would glorify God* (John 21:18–19).

Peter's faith was strong and in time his courage grew to match his faith. History records that Peter was crucified for his faith. According to tradition, Peter insisted on being crucified upside down because he felt unworthy to die in the same manner as his Lord.

Like Peter, we can triumph over our fear! The death and resurrection of Christ sets us free to live our new life unhindered by the fears that characterize the old life. The presence and power of God in us through the Holy Spirit can banish the fear that so often seems to control us. The more we love and trust the Lord, the less power fear will have over us.

God's Word Conquers Fear

Knowledge of and faithful obedience to the Word of God are very important factors in overcoming fear. Learning to trust and rely on God's Word can help us become conquerors in any situation. We see this demonstrated in the life of Daniel and his three friends.

Despite the fact that he was a servant in a foreign land, Daniel let the Word of God make him the conqueror. Nebuchadnezzar, king of Babylon, had overcome Jerusalem. Daniel and three of his friends, Hananiah, Mishael, and Azariah, being of the royal tribe of Judah, were among the first captured. The Bible records how handsome, smart, and accomplished they were—young men of excellent character, wise beyond their years, and poised enough to stand before kings.

As they were being groomed to enter the king's service, they were assigned a special diet and received a special education. In an effort to change their identities, the king ordered that they be given new names: *"Then the commander of the officials assigned new names to them; and to Daniel he assigned the name Belteshazzar, to Hananiah Shadrach, to Mishael Meshach and to Azariah Abed-nego"* (Daniel 1:7).

The new diet would require these faithful Jewish men to violate the dietary laws that they had grown up with, and they were determined not to let that happen:

> *But Daniel made up his mind that he would not defile himself with the king's choice food or with the wine which he drank; so he sought*

> *permission from the commander of the officials that he might not defile himself. Now God granted Daniel favor and compassion in the sight of the commander of the officials* (Daniel 1:8–9).

Daniel and his friends refused to change their image and identity in order to serve a foreign "god." Instead, they honored God's Word by arranging an alternative that would not require them to disobey the Lord. Daniel proposed a test:

> *But Daniel said to the overseer whom the commander of the officials had appointed over Daniel, Hananiah, Mishael and Azariah, "Please test your servants for ten days, and let us be given some vegetables to eat and water to drink. Then let our appearance be observed in your presence and the appearance of the youths who are eating the king's choice food; and deal with your servants according to what you see." So he listened to them in this matter and tested them for ten days. At the end of ten days their appearance seemed better and they were fatter than all the youths who had been eating the king's choice food* (Daniel 1:11–15).

The Bible says that as a result of their faithfulness, God gave Daniel, Hananiah, Mishael, and Azariah greater wisdom and understanding than anyone else in the kingdom, and they became the king's choicest advisors. A circumstance that could have overcome them with fear became their arena of conquest as they overcame their fear through faithfulness to God's Word.

Prayer Conquers Fear

Prayer is another essential weapon for overcoming fear! Again we see this in the life of Daniel and his friends. Once, when King Nebuchadnezzar had a puzzling dream that he could not understand, he became furious when his magicians, conjurers, and sorcerers could not interpret his dream. In his anger, he ordered that all the wise men of the kingdom be put to death. This decree included Daniel and his friends.

Instead of giving in to fear, however, Daniel and the others called a prayer meeting:

> *Then Daniel went to his house and informed his friends, Hananiah, Mishael and Azariah, about the matter, so that they might request compassion from the God of heaven concerning this mystery, so that Daniel and his friends would not be destroyed with the rest of the wise men of Babylon. Then the mystery was revealed to Daniel in a night vision* (Daniel 2:17–19).

As a result of this prayer, God gave Daniel understanding of the king's dream as well as its meaning. Daniel went before the king, explained the king's dream, and saved all the kingdom's wise men from death. When the king saw the discernment and wisdom of Daniel, he promoted him, and Daniel, the slave, became one of the most powerful men in the kingdom: *"Then the king promoted Daniel and gave him many great gifts, and he made him ruler over the whole province of Babylon and chief prefect over all the wise men of Babylon"* (Daniel 2:48).

"We never know what great things God may do in our world because we pray."

This prayer meeting was not an isolated event for Daniel. Prayer came as naturally to him as breathing. The Bible says that Daniel prayed regularly three times a day—first thing in the morning, at noon, and the last thing at night.

The lesson in this for us is that Christians should have a disciplined and faithful prayer life. We never know what great things God may do in our world because we pray.

A few years back my husband, Wally, initiated early morning prayer sessions at our church. He "selected" the 5 a.m. sessions for himself and me. As the alarm rang at 4:30 a.m., I could not imagine how I would ever make it. Yet, I knew that both my husband and God wanted me to go.

I began to claim Hebrews 11:6 that God rewards those who diligently seek Him—even at five o'clock in the morning. God rewarded us for our diligence: That year we saw literally hundreds and hundreds of answers to prayer. Now Wally leads a group every Monday evening and the lives of many in our church are being transformed as they follow his example of diligent intercession.

Daniel had circumstances in his life that could have driven him to despair and defeat: slavery, fear of death, separation from family and friends. Had he allowed it, fear could have driven out Daniel's faith. Instead, he stayed strong in his trust of the Lord and overcame his fear.

Years ago Wally and I had a personal experience that demonstrated the power of prayer to overcome fear. When our son Mike was six years old, a mentally disturbed woman kidnapped him from a playground. It was a very frightening experience! At the very moment we realized what had happened, my husband grabbed my hand to pray. He said, "Marilyn, we're going to believe that Mike will be safely returned to us in one hour."

The police told us they had a report of a woman taking a little boy from the playground. We were speaking to a police officer at the playground when I looked down the street and saw a woman three blocks away who was walking with a small boy.

"That's our son!" I shouted. Jumping into his squad car, the officer told us to wait. He drove those three blocks, picked up Mike and the woman who had taken him, and returned to where we were waiting. As Mike got out of the police car, I looked at my watch—exactly one hour had passed since Wally and I prayed for Mike's safe return! Instead of giving in to fear, we prayed and gave our fear to the Lord. He was faithful to hear and answer our prayers! Prayer can overcome fear.

Don't Let Go of the Word!

Fear is the greatest enemy of all to your faith. If Satan can fill you with fear he can control every aspect of your life. As fearful as life can be at times, you do not have to be at the mercy of fear. As long as you hold on stubbornly to the Word of God and to prayer, fear will not be able to get a stranglehold on you. God's Word is alive! Let it guide you to complete freedom from fear.

First, don't focus on your circumstances. Focus instead on God's Word. By continually looking to God, you will be filled with faith. Repeat the Word; say it over and over and you will replace fear with God's truth. (See Philippians 1:14.)

Second, praise God. Thank Him for His goodness and worship Him. Give a "sacrifice of praise" in the midst of your terrible circumstances. Say, "Lord, I praise and thank You that I am victorious, that I am delivered, and that I am set free. I thank You that all my needs are met according to Your riches in glory by Christ Jesus." Praising God will overcome fear. (See Psalm 27.)

Third, act: Do what you know God wants you to do. Is there something God told you to do or something you have vowed to do? Then do it! It may be something as simple as not murmuring. Whatever God tells you to do, act on the Word and do it! (See James 1:22–25.)

Fourth and finally, confess that you are delivered *now*! Pray the Word and believe in the answer. As Jesus said to Jairus before his daughter was raised from death, *"Do not be afraid; only believe"* (Mark 5:36 NKJV). Only believe! That is the hallmark of simple, childlike faith that knows no fear because its trust is in the God who cannot fail. There is no fear in love because perfect love casts out fear. Banish your fear with faith! Whatever your circumstances, don't be afraid! Like the little girl standing on the chair, leap into your Daddy's arms. He will catch you!

STEPS TO A SIMPLER FAITH

1. Look in a Bible concordance and write down three verses that say we can "put the enemy to flight."
2. Perfect love casts out all fear. Remember times in your past when the love of God or others has delivered you from a fearful situation. Share these times with a friend.
3. Look at these four types of fear and find Scriptures to help you overcome them:
   - Fear of physical illness
   - Fear of circumstances
   - Fear of man
   - Fear of the world around you
4. Find godly people who have the boldness to do what God has called them to do. Ask them how God has helped them to overcome fear.

5. Daniel is a great example of a godly person with high morals and strong character. List five attributes of his character that you would like to have. Pray, ask, and believe God for them.

CHAPTER SIX

Triumph Over Tests, Trials, and Temptations

Childhood is a time of learning, with adulthood and maturity as the end goal. Learning always carries its share of tests, trials, and temptations. Children must learn to talk. They must learn to walk, with lots of falls, bumps, and bruises along the way. Later, they learn to ride a bicycle—with all of *its* falls, bumps, and bruises. Children must learn the importance of honesty, integrity, telling the truth, and taking responsibility for their actions and decisions.

Then there is school, with its pressure to get good—or at least passing—grades. School is also where temptations of all kinds abound: to lie, to cheat, to use profanity, to smoke, to drink, to take drugs. In order for children to triumph over the tests and trials of childhood, they need to know that they are not alone in the struggle—that mature, caring people who love them and who they trust are there to help them through.

Faith is the same way. The Christian life is a journey to maturity, with plenty of bumps, bruises, tests, trials, and temptations along the way. Maturity does not mean letting go of childlikeness, but it does mean laying aside *childishness*. Childishness is a mark of immaturity. Paul wrote, *"When I was a child, I used to speak like a child, think like a child, reason like a child; when I became a man, I did away with childish things*" (1 Corinthians 13:11).

Where faith is concerned, childlikeness is a sign of maturity. The more childlike we become in our faith and in our approach to our Christian walk, the more mature we become. Children depend on their parents and other responsible, caring adults to protect them, care for them, and help them make it through the trials of childhood and become mature, responsible adults. People of childlike faith know that they must depend on their heavenly Father to protect them, care for them, and help them triumph in their trials because they know they do not have the strength or wisdom to do it on their own.

"Where faith is concerned, childlikeness is a sign of maturity."

Most of us don't like the thought of facing tests or trials, but they are an inescapable part of life. I have been through many trials and expect to go through many more. Rather than thinking of trials and tests only as bad things to be avoided, we need to understand that many times they serve God's purpose in shaping us into the people He wants us to be. As James observed:

> *Blessed (happy, to be envied) is the man who is patient under trial and stands up under temptation, for when he has stood the test and been approved, he will receive [the victor's] crown of life which God has promised to those who love Him* (James 1:12 AMP).

Have you been trusting God for a provision or even a miracle in some area of your life yet feel as though the answer is as far away as it was when you started? Are you in the midst of some test or trial and cannot yet see the end of it? Don't let your current troubles convince you that your faith is not working. The presence of trials is a sure sign that God is working in your life. He is either chastening you in order to lead you to repent of sins in your life, or else He is using the trial to mature you and to prepare you for greater things:

> *You should know in your heart that as a man chastens his son, so the LORD your God chastens you* (Deuteronomy 8:5 NKJV).

> *"For whom the* Lord *loves He chastens, and scourges every son whom He receives." If you endure chastening, God deals with you as with sons; for what son is there whom a father does not chasten?* (Hebrews 12:6–7 NKJV)

> *My brethren, count it all joy when you fall into various trials, knowing that the testing of your faith produces patience. But let patience have its perfect work, that you may be perfect and complete, lacking nothing* (James 1:2–4 NKJV)

There is an important spiritual principle at work here: God only promotes you when you successfully complete the present grade level. Like a patient tutor who will not take his student to a new lesson until he learns the current one, God works with you through your trials until you learn to trust Him in your current situation. Not only does He want you to trust Him to bring you through, He also wants you to face your trials with *joy*!

Why be *joyful* about your trials? They prove that God is working in your life, taking personal interest in your development as a Father who loves and delights in His children. Trials are temporary and give way to eternal rewards and benefits. The point is not so much to take joy in the trials themselves as in what they are producing in you in the way of maturity and faith. If you are facing great trials today, hang in there; great blessings are just around the corner!

> *Sing praise to the* Lord, *you His godly ones, and give thanks to His holy name. For His anger is but for a moment, His favor is for a lifetime; weeping may last for the night, but a shout of joy comes in the morning* (Psalm 30:4–5).

You Are Stronger Than You Think

No one likes to go through hard times, but coming out the other side of a trial in victory demonstrates God's grace and power. Think back to when God brought you through earlier hard times. Do you remember those moments in the midst of your troubles when you thought they would never end and that you would never survive? Well, here you are today. You made it. What God did before He will do again;

simply trust Him. Learning to "rehearse" your past victories of faith will strengthen you to face current trials. As James says, when your faith is tested, you will learn to endure, and endurance results in maturity. To endure means to remain firm under suffering or misfortune without yielding; to bear patiently. Endurance is the ability to withstand hardship, adversity, or stress.

Many times in the Bible a "test" or "trial" refers not to a negative or destructive event but to a positive process of pruning or refining to produce a purer and better product: *"For You, O God, have tested us; You have refined us as silver is refined"* (Psalm 66:10 NKJV). Testing "proves" and improves your faith. Every time you take a God-kind of step in your trial, you become stronger.

With Christ in your life and the Holy Spirit in your heart, you are stronger than you think you are. Never forget, however, that it is *His* strength, not yours, that makes you strong. The more you learn to trust God in your trials, the more childlike your faith becomes because you are depending on God and not on yourself. Childlike faith is the kind of faith that brings victory: *"For whatever is born of God overcomes the world; and this is the victory that has overcome the world—our faith"* (1 John 5:4).

"Testing 'proves' and improves your faith."

Trials often test our faith in God's Word. Have you ever gone hiking in the mountains and had your foot slip and slide back down the path? In the same way, if you are not careful, a trial can cause you to "slip" in your faith and fail to trust God. Be encouraged, for the Word says that your *"foot stands on a level place"* (Psalm 26:12). When you stand on God's Word, you are safe and secure. Take the Word into your trial and you will be victorious every time. When you face a trial in your own strength, you may be tempted to give up. Instead, stick with the Word of God and learn to overcome.

Once, when our ministry was going through a terrible financial trial, the devil told me to close the doors. He said that I had never been capable of making good financial decisions—that I had blown it. God didn't say that to me; in fact, God gave me a promise that if I would trust Him, He would bring me through. While my staff was worried, I stood on the Word. I said, "God will deliver us; God is delivering us," and within one month, we had a total financial turnaround. When the road ahead looks impossible, put your confidence in God and His Word. Faith will keep you steady until your circumstances come into line with what God said.

One of the challenges we face as Christians seeking to grow in our faith is that we live in a world that rejects and opposes God. Every day we encounter ideas, philosophies, attitudes, and lifestyles that are contrary to what God has revealed in His Word. These influences are often so subtle and pervasive that if we are not careful they will insinuate their way into our hearts until they form a stronghold in our life that resists the Spirit of God.

The word *stronghold*, as used in the Bible, means "any fortified place" where we are not letting God teach and change us. We may receive deliverance from a sin or problem only to have it return time after time because we did not totally destroy its hold in our lives and replace it with a fortress of God's Word. Life then becomes like a yo-yo, going up and down between victory and defeat, fighting the same battle over and over—constantly repeating the same test. The Bible says we do not have to live that way. On the contrary, we can live in continuous freedom. Jesus said, *"If you continue in My word, then you are truly disciples of Mine; and you will know the truth, and the truth will make you free"* (John 8:31–32).

The Word of the Lord is the Word of truth, and that truth can set you free from any stronghold of sin in your life. You are stronger than you think because He who lives in you is greater than he who lives in the world (see 1 John 4:4). If you learn to apply the weapons God has given you—the weapons of faith and His Word—no trial or stronghold will be able to stand against you. Consider the words of the apostle Paul:

> *For though we live in the world, we do not wage war as the world does. The weapons we fight with are not the weapons of the world. On the contrary, they have divine power to demolish strongholds. We demolish arguments and every pretension that sets itself up against the knowledge of God, and we take captive every thought to make it obedient to Christ* (2 Corinthians 10:3–5 NIV).

Facing trials and temptations on your own is daunting, which is why God gave you a helper—the Holy Spirit. Learning to pray in the Spirit will give you a special power boost; plus, it will remind you that you need never go through your trials alone:

> *In the same way the Spirit also helps our weakness; for we do not know how to pray as we should, but the Spirit Himself intercedes for us with groanings too deep for words; and He who searches the hearts knows what the mind of the Spirit is, because He intercedes for the saints according to the will of God* (Romans 8:26–27).

The Holy Spirit prays for you according to God's perfect will. Have you ever found yourself in the midst of a trial and so flustered and upset that you couldn't even think straight, much less have any clue how to pray? Always, but especially in times like those, the Holy Spirit Himself intercedes for us. Regardless of how difficult your trial may seem, in the end, everything will work together for good. That is God's promise.

Learn Your Lessons

In many ways, growing in faith is like being in school. The Holy Spirit is your teacher and the Word of God is your textbook. Sometimes learning the lessons is hard because of outside distractions. As soon as you get serious about following the Lord and learning His ways, the devil will do everything he can to make things hard for you. Like a mean classroom bully, Satan will try to keep you from learning and growing in faith by mocking you, tempting you, making you feel stupid, and by trying to cause you to doubt God and His goodness. He will send many temptations your way, but if you fill your mind with the Word of God, those temptations will become nothing more than a bully's blustering. Learn to think of each test that comes as an opportunity to prove to yourself, the world, and the devil that you have learned your lesson: God's Word really does work! Even if you feel defeated, stand up in faith and tell Satan that the game is not over—you are playing until you win!

The key to victory, however, is humble submission to the Lord. You cannot defeat the bully by yourself. You need the help of someone bigger and stronger than you are. Submission is a childlike act. It demonstrates trust, respect for authority, and recognition of personal weakness and the need for help from someone stronger. No one is bigger and stronger than God is. Focus your attention on God and His power, not on the devil:

> *"Submit yourselves, then, to God. Resist the devil, and he will flee from you. Come near to God and he will come near to you"* (James 4:7–8 NIV).

As you seek to grow in faith and draw closer to the Lord, be prepared for fierce and fiery attacks from the devil. Some are designed to harass you while others are intended to destroy your life and ministry. Use your faith to quench the fire:

> *In addition to all, taking up the shield of faith with which you will be able to extinguish all the flaming arrows of the evil one* (Ephesians 6:16).

> *No temptation has overtaken you but such as is common to man; and God is faithful, who will not allow you to be tempted beyond what you are able, but with the temptation will provide the way of escape also, so that you will be able to endure it* (1 Corinthians 10:13).

How do you take *"up the shield of faith"*? What is the *"way of escape"* that God has provided? The answer to both questions is the same: the Word of God. Remember that *"faith comes by hearing, and hearing by the word of God"* (Romans 10:17 NKJV). The truths of God's Word will fend off and quench the fiery lies of the devil and will give you the strength of wisdom to resist and endure temptation.

Don't let Satan, the classroom bully, tell you that you can't accomplish your purpose or that you are a loser. Remind yourself that you have divine energy and ability. Satan will try to deceive you by telling you that you are too sickly, too stupid, too weak, or too old to do what God has said to do. He will try to convince you to give up the fight. Don't listen to his lies or threats. When you are filled with the Holy Spirit, you have all the wisdom, strength, and energy you need to obey God and accomplish His purpose.

Remember who your real Daddy is. Your position as a child of God entitles you to go to the "head of the class"! Get an image into your mind of yourself as a lawful heir to good things, and then claim your inheritance! The Holy Spirit Himself will tell you who you are:

> *Those who are led by the Spirit of God are sons of God. For you did not receive a spirit that makes you a slave again to fear, but you received the Spirit of sonship. And by him we cry, "Abba, Father." The Spirit himself testifies with our spirit that we are God's children. Now*

if we are children, then we are heirs—heirs of God and co-heirs with Christ (Romans 8:14–17 NIV).

"When you have the Holy Spirit, you have all you need to obey God and accomplish His purpose."

Satan particularly likes to strike when we are weary or worn down. One time, when we were going through some hard trials and I was very tired, the devil spoke to me: "You are having a nervous breakdown just like your father did. Why don't you just commit suicide right now?" That thought was so strong and overwhelming that I instantly cried out to God. "God, help me! Help me! I'm just like my father and I'm having a nervous breakdown!"

Just as quickly, the Lord answered, "You *are* just like your Father, that's true. *I* am your Father, and I have never had a nervous breakdown, so you won't, either." Don't let Satan fill your heart with lies and fear; trust God and He will deliver you through every trial.

Because he has loved Me, therefore I will deliver him; I will set him securely on high, because he has known My name. He will call upon Me, and I will answer him; I will be with him in trouble; I will rescue him and honor him (Psalm 91:14–15).

Watch Out for Counterfeits

Sometimes during a trial, while you are waiting for God's provision, Satan will offer you a counterfeit answer. Under the circumstances it may look pretty good and be quite appealing on the surface, but yet it is not in line with the Word or will of God. This is exactly the ploy that Satan used to tempt Jesus in the wilderness. Three times the devil offered Jesus a less demanding and more ego-feeding "alternative" to the plan Jesus received from His Father. Each of these alternatives would have enabled Jesus to avoid the cross. The cross, however, was absolutely essential to God's plan to save mankind from sin. Wisely, Jesus rejected these counterfeit alternatives and stayed focused on His Father's will. He did this by measuring each "alternative" against the unchanging standard of God's Word and exposing them for the counterfeits they were.

Jesus was tested in other ways as well:

> *The Pharisees and Sadducees came up, and testing Jesus, they asked Him to show them a sign from heaven. But He replied to them..."An evil and adulterous generation seeks after a sign; and a sign will not be given it, except the sign of Jonah"* (Matthew 16:1–2, 4).

> *Then the Pharisees went and plotted together how they might trap Him in what He said...."Tell us then, what do You think? Is it lawful to give a poll-tax to Caesar, or not?" But Jesus perceived their malice, and said, "Why are you testing Me, you hypocrites?...Render to Caesar the things that are Caesar's; and to God the things that are God's"* (Matthew 22:15, 17–18, 21).

All of these tests obviously were not from God, but because of them Jesus is able to help us pass ours! How did Jesus resist temptation? How did He pass the tests? His secret weapon was the Word of God. Because He faced—and overcame—temptation, He can help us do the same:

> *For we do not have a high priest who cannot sympathize with our weaknesses, but One who has been tempted in all things as we are, yet without sin* (Hebrews 4:15).

> *For since He Himself was tempted in that which He has suffered, He is able to come to the aid of those who are tempted* (Hebrews 2:18).

When you are under the stress and pressure of a trial, the temptation to take the easy way out can become overwhelming. Remember, God will *never* go against His Word. If an "answer" lies before you that contradicts the Word of God, you can be sure that it did *not* come from God. Don't fall for Satan's counterfeit. Be patient and wait for God's answer. Study His Word and seek to learn what He has to say about your situation. Better yet, establish and follow a daily reading plan that will take you through the entire Bible once a year. Such a discipline will provide you with a steady supply of the Word to support you during any trial.

Wait for the Real Thing

Long ago, Abraham fell for a counterfeit provision. God had promised him an heir, a son by his wife, Sarah. Both Abraham and Sarah were beyond normal child-bearing age, and when Sarah failed to conceive, they became impatient. Finally, Sarah suggested that Abraham have a son by Hagar, her Egyptian maid. Thus, Ishmael was born. Ishmael was not the child of promise, however; he was a counterfeit! Although Ishmael was blessed in many ways, he was not the true heir. In due time, God did fulfill His promise to Abraham, and Isaac was born (see Genesis 16 and 21).

As appealing or sensible as a counterfeit may appear, following it is dangerous. When Abraham and Sarah took matters into their own hands to produce Ishmael, it probably seemed like a sensible and reasonable course of action. Historically, however, it proved to be a decision with serious consequences. Throughout the centuries, the descendants of Ishmael and the descendants of Isaac have been at odds with each other. Today we see this in the ongoing conflict between the Arabs and the Jews.

It is easy to fall into the trap of taking matters into your own hands. Have you ever tried to "help" God out and ended up missing your miracle? I have! Waiting for the promise can make you wonder if it was even in God's plan in the first place. Rest assured, if God makes a promise in His Word, it is His will and He will bring it to pass. Even if His answer is delayed, His timing is always perfect.

Sometimes waiting for God to answer or bring you through a trial is really hard to do. Pressure mounts until you feel like giving up. That is when you must decide whether to hold on and keep believing God's promise or surrender and give the devil the victory.

My advice to you is to hold on to your confession, hope against hope, and continue to believe the promise that God will see you through. Keep His Word in your mouth and in your mind and heart and eventually you will obtain the fulfillment of the promise. God's promises are as certain as the sun rising in the east. Do not walk by what you see, but walk by faith:

> *For no matter how many promises God has made, they are "Yes" in Christ. And so through him the "Amen" is spoken by us to the glory of God. Now it is God who makes both us and you stand firm in Christ. He anointed us, set his seal of ownership on us, and put his Spirit in our hearts as a deposit, guaranteeing what is to come* (2 Corinthians 1:20–22 NIV).

God allows tests to come, but He never allows us to be tested beyond our ability to endure. Our endurance depends on His strength and provision, not our own. If we try in our own strength, we will fail every time. Whenever God sends or allows tests, He has our best at heart.

Another event from the life of Abraham shows how God sometimes sends this kind of test. In this case, God wanted to "prove" Abraham—to test his faith. God asked Abraham to sacrifice his son Isaac—the son through whom God's promise was to be fulfilled. Abraham never flinched. In complete faith and obedience he made all the preparations necessary to carry out God's command. Taking his son Isaac, Abraham traveled to a certain mountain where he built an altar. After binding Isaac and placing him on the altar, Abraham raised his knife, ready to slay his son as a burnt offering to God. It was at that point that God stayed his hand. Abraham had passed the test:

> "God's promises are as certain as the sun rising in the east."

> *He said, "Do not stretch out your hand against the lad, and do nothing to him; for now I know that you fear God, since you have not withheld your son, your only son, from Me." Then Abraham raised his eyes and looked, and behold, behind him a ram caught in the thicket by his horns; and Abraham went and took the ram and offered him up for a burnt offering in the place of his son. Abraham called the name of that place The Lord Will Provide, as it is said to this day, "In the mount of the Lord it will be provided"* (Genesis 22:12–14).

Watch out for counterfeits. A counterfeit "solution" to your trial will only lead you away from the Lord and His Word, and it may make your situation even worse. Your trial may be God's way of testing, proving, or refining your faith. Wait for *His* answer; it will draw you closer to Him and lead you to victory.

The Choice Is Yours

Although you may have little control over the trials and temptations that come into your life, you *do* have control over how you respond to them. On the one hand, you can dwell on your temptations and indulge them. You can complain about your trials, and fuss and fight and fume and let yourself get beaten up left and right.

On the other hand, you can turn to God and His Word for wisdom to make the right decisions and the strength to endure. You can submit yourself to God, then resist the devil and watch him flee. You can seek God's face in the midst of your trial and humbly ask Him to teach you and strengthen you in the midst of it.

In the end, it all comes down to who you listen to. In the Garden of Eden, Eve listened to the voice of the serpent—*big* mistake! Satan whispered to her, flattered her, fed her ego, and placed doubts in her mind regarding God's goodness and truthfulness. Adam listened to Eve. By the time Satan was finished, he had persuaded both of them to doubt God. Doubt led to disobedience, and disobedience led to disaster—all from listening to the wrong voice.

Don't make the same mistake Adam and Eve made. Satan will try to use the same tactics on you. When you are at a crossroads in your life, trying to endure a trial or believing for a promise or a miracle, Satan will whisper in your ear: "Are you *sure* God really wants you to do that?" "Did God *really* say that He would provide all your needs?" "How do you *know* you can trust Him?" "He's not interested in someone who has messed up as much as you have! Who do you think you are?" These are all lies designed to weaken your faith and cause you to doubt God. Don't fall for them. Keep your heart and mind focused on God's Word. His promises never fail.

Children who fail in school sometimes have to repeat the same grade. Diligent teachers hold them back because they want the student to learn the material and be successful. Likewise, God is a diligent teacher and He often will keep us traveling along the same roads until we learn the lesson!

The children of Israel went through numerous trials, failing one test after another. Why? Perhaps they were too busy complaining about their trials to see the hand of God at work in their lives. After they crossed the Red Sea, the people were jubilant—filled with faith and trust in God. Soon, however, they had a new test: lack of water. They should have responded in faith. "If God can part the Red Sea, He can easily supply water for us." Instead, they murmured and complained, questioning Moses and God. Despite their bad attitudes, God honored

Moses' prayers and turned the bitter waters of Marah into sweet water, and He provided twelve springs of water and seventy date palms. (See Exodus 15:23–27.)

In the very next chapter of Exodus we read that the children of Israel went through another trial: lack of food. They could have said, "Our God just supplied abundant water for us, so we know He will provide food!" Instead, they complained. Does that describe you? Are you wandering in a wilderness of trials and tribulations? Do you constantly complain about your lot and never remember all that God has done for you in the past?

The Israelites could have been in the Promised Land less than a year after leaving Egypt. Instead, that first generation never got there at all. The Lord said to Moses:

> *Surely all the men who have seen My glory and My signs which I performed in Egypt and in the wilderness, yet have put Me to the test these ten times and have not listened to My voice, shall by no means see the land which I swore to their fathers, nor shall any of those who spurned Me see it* (Numbers 14:22–23).

What went wrong? The Israelites had a bad attitude and their problems overwhelmed them. Their example demonstrates an important principle: either defeat your problems or they will defeat you. When it comes to testing, you basically have three choices:

1. Complain, and take the test over again.
2. Complain, give up, and totally miss God's promises and provision.
3. Praise God, stand on His Word, pass the test, and enter your promised land!

Which would *you* choose?

Perhaps you feel that you have messed up so many times in the past that there is no use trying to change things. Your life seems to be an unbroken chain of problems—one trial after another. If so, have you humbled yourself before God and asked Him to show you what needs to change in your life or your words or your attitude? Your past does not have to determine your future. You can break the cycle. Simply learn to speak the Word of God in faith, act on the Word in obedience, and trust God.

In Christ, your past failures mean nothing:

> *Therefore there is now no condemnation for those who are in Christ Jesus. For the law of the Spirit of life in Christ Jesus has set you free from the law of sin and of death* (Romans 8:1–2).

God says your past failures are forever forgotten. This means you are free from attacks on your mind and character! You now live under a higher law, the law of Spirit and life! Overcome every temptation by setting your mind on godly things. You don't have to live with guilt or self-pity, or fall prey to Satan's lies about you. Sin has no power over you and neither does temptation. Temptation is not sin—as long as you resist it in the power of the Spirit. Purpose in your heart to give the Holy Spirit complete control of your life. He will always help you overcome temptation and live a life of peace.

"The key to victory is to keep your eyes focused on the Lord."

Stay Fixed on Jesus

How do you overcome tests, trials, and temptations? Don't focus on the apparent size or strength of the problem, and don't try to win in your own strength. The key to victory is to keep your eyes focused on the Lord, who is your source of strength and power. Children often learn by watching their parents. In the same way, we learn to be like Jesus by watching Him and doing what He did. The writer of Hebrews said:

> *Therefore, since we have so great a cloud of witnesses surrounding us, let us also lay aside every encumbrance and the sin which so easily entangles us, and let us run with endurance the race that is set before us, fixing our eyes on Jesus, the author and perfecter of faith, who for the joy set before Him endured the cross, despising the shame, and has sat down at the right hand of the throne of God* (Hebrews 12:1–2).

Some Christians experience a great victory only to have a harder trial rise up immediately afterward. In some cases this is a counterattack by the enemy, but in others it is the result of their letting their guard down and allowing themselves to depend on someone or something other than God. Be very careful about this! If God is not your source for everything, you are stepping into the devil's territory.

When you come safely and successfully through a temptation or trial (and you will), continue to build on your victory. Don't allow yourself to become complacent. Once you pull down a stronghold of sin or evil, be sure to erect a stronghold or fortress of the Word of God in its place. The book of James provides three practical steps in this process that will help you neutralize an attack of the enemy:

1. *Look ahead.* Watch out for "good-looking" bait disguising the hidden hook of sin. Consider the consequences of sin—death. Don't take the bait! *"Do not be deceived, my beloved brethren"* (James 1:16).

2. *Look around.* See and proclaim the goodness of God. He has provision for your every need. When you meet temptation, say, "Why give in to that trap? God has much better things for me." He wants you to have a miracle! *"Every good thing given and every perfect gift is from above, coming down from the Father of lights, with whom there is no variation or shifting shadow"* (James 1:17).

3. *Look within* to the nature of Jesus Christ. See that you are clothed with His righteousness. When God looks at you, He says, "You are the best! You have My nature within." *"In the exercise of His will He brought us forth by the word of truth, so that we would be a kind of first fruits among His creatures"* (James 1:18).

Once you know what lies ahead—what miracles and blessings are yours in the future—suddenly the trial or test you are going through now won't seem as difficult to bear. Instead of giving into murmuring, speak the Word. During your trials, remember that while God has prepared a miracle for the "outside," He also wants to do a work on the "inside" as well:

> *Consider it all joy, my brethren, when you encounter various trials, knowing that the testing of your faith produces endurance. And let endurance have its perfect result, so that you may be perfect and complete, lacking in nothing* (James 1:2–4).

Not only does God want to bring you a miracle, He is even more interested in building your character. When you rely totally on the integrity of God's Word and trust Him in all things, including your trials, you will acquire maturity in your Christian walk. You must be patient, never diverting your eyes from what God has promised. Then you will become "perfect" or "mature," and lack for nothing.

STEPS TO A SIMPLER FAITH

1. Name some of the tests that came upon the children of Israel because of their lack of faith in God.
2. Think of a stronghold in your own life. What Bible promises can you find to use as a barrier against the lies of the devil?
3. List at least three positive ways you can respond to a test or temptation.
4. What do "joy" and "patience" have to do with testing? Do you know anyone who is joyful or patient from whom you could learn?
5. Meditate on James 1:16–18. Pray about how to apply this truth to a trial you are facing.

CHAPTER SEVEN

Use Your God-Given Authority

An important part of a mature yet childlike faith is understanding the proper place, use, and limits of authority. Very young children have little or no authority because they are too young and inexperienced to know what to do with it. Parents and other adults in authority over them tell them where to go and what to do, when and what to eat, what to wear, and so forth. As children grow, they normally learn to accept greater amounts of authority and responsibility for their own decisions and actions. The final goal is for them to become responsible, self-directed adults who know how to properly exercise authority over those who are under them and respect the authority of those who are over them.

What authority do you exercise in your life? Perhaps you are in a position of authority on your job, supervising or managing other employees. If you are a parent of small children, hopefully you exercise authority over them for their own good, protection, and welfare. Who looks to you for instruction, inspiration, or guidance? Are you a mentor or "hero" to anyone? Whose lives do you influence by your example?

Did you know that as a Christian you have great authority in this world? All of us who claim the name of Christ have received authority from Him to act in His name and for His kingdom. In other words, we have *delegated authority*—authority that we exercise not as free agents, but as Christ's representatives. One of the best biblical examples of this delegated authority is found in the "Great Commission" at the end of Matthew's Gospel:

> *And Jesus came up and spoke to them, saying, "All authority has been given to Me in heaven and on earth. Go therefore and make disciples of all the nations, baptizing them in the name of the Father and the Son and the Holy Spirit, teaching them to observe all that I commanded you; and lo, I am with you always, even to the end of the age"* (Matthew 28:18–20).

Jesus has all authority and He commands us to go *in* His authority and *with* His authority to *"make disciples of all the nations."* The authority we have is not our own but *His* authority that He has delegated to us. That is a critical point to remember if we want to properly understand and exercise authority in the spiritual realm.

Created to Rule the Earth

If you have a problem with service in a restaurant, who do you demand to see? If there is a mistake on your phone bill that customer service cannot or will not fix, who do you turn to? When you are in a bind or really need to get something done, who do you go to? You ask for the "person in charge"—the person with *authority*.

When God created this world, He intended for mankind to be "in charge" of it:

> *Then God said, "Let Us make man in Our image, according to Our likeness; and let them rule over the fish of the sea and over the birds of the sky and over the cattle and over all the earth, and over every creeping thing that creeps on the earth"* (Genesis 1:26).

Have you ever considered the fact that you were created to rule the earth? From the beginning, God set apart the world as our domain: *"The heavens are the heavens of the Lord, but the earth He has given to the sons of men"* (Psalm 115:16).

God created Adam and told him to fill and subdue the earth. The Hebrew word for "subdue" is *kabash*, which means "to conquer, subjugate, bring into bondage, force, keep under, bring into subjection." Just as man is subject to God's authority, the created order was made to be subject to man's authority: *"You make him to rule over the works of Your hands; You have put all things under his feet"* (Psalm 8:6).

When it came to man, God formed him out of the existing earth—the *"dust of the ground"* (Genesis 2:7 NKJV)—and then breathed into him the breath of life. Later on, God put the man to sleep, took a part of his side, and made a woman. In God's eyes, as with all the rest of His creation, the man and woman were "very good." Adam and Eve had God's image, God's authority, and God's wisdom. Their complete identity was in Him!

Everything was perfect. God had provided Adam with a perfect home, a beautiful wife, and a wonderful job taking care of a glorious garden! Adam had intelligence that surpasses anything we know today. Not only did he name all the animals, but he also remembered their names! He had perfect recall.

Then trouble set in. Satan could not stand the fact that God had given Adam authority over the world and its creatures. Having been thrown out of heaven, Satan wanted earthly authority for himself so that he could become the "god of this world." Immediately, he set out to usurp the authority that rightly belonged to man. The father of lies lied to Eve, casting doubt and uncertainty in her heart:

> *Then the serpent said to the woman, "You will not surely die. For God knows that in the day you eat of it your eyes will be opened, and you will be like God, knowing good and evil"* (Genesis 3:4–5 NKJV).

Use It or Lose It!

Wait a minute! Do you see the devil's deception? God had *already* made Adam and Eve in His image. They were *already* like Him! Adam and Eve had their authority, their power, their position—indeed, their complete identity—in God. By tempting them to doubt God, Satan was also tempting them to question their identity. He will try to do the same with you.

Satan wants to steal two things from you: the authority of God's Word in your life and your identity in God's life. He wants to make you think that you are a "nobody," alone and powerless. His goal is to convince you to act independently of God and move outside His authority. When Satan acted independently of God to gain his own authority, he lost it all. Now, he wants you to do the same thing. Don't fall for it! Your authority rests in God alone—not apart from Him!

God gave Adam the authority to guard and protect the garden. Adam should have used his God-given authority to drive out the serpent, to stop him from speaking contrary to God's Word, and to warn his wife. By refusing to use his authority, he lost it!

Has Satan tried to play the same trick on you? Has the father of lies tried to convince you that you are a nobody? Have you found yourself at times questioning whether God will really answer your prayers? Don't let Satan steal your authority!

Once I was on a plane going to Albany, New York, for a special church service. Before the plane departed the pilot announced that we would be two hours late. My heart dropped. If we were late, I would miss the service. Then the Lord spoke to me, "You know, you have authority in the name of Jesus." I began to bind the enemy from hindering the plane's departure.

"Your authority rests in God alone—not apart from Him."

Within fifteen minutes, the pilot said, "Well, it was not as big a problem as we thought, and we will be taking off shortly." We arrived in time for the service. The authority of Jesus is bigger than a delayed plane; it is bigger than any problem Satan can throw at you. Don't fall for the same deception that fooled Adam and Eve. You have been given authority over the devil by God Himself. Use it!

Adam and Eve paid a terrible price for their mistake. They lost their dominion—the earth—by disobeying God. Though created in the image of God, Adam and Eve had taken on a strange, evil nature—the nature of sin. They lost their perfect home in the Garden of Eden and had to cultivate ordinary ground and work hard for everything they ate. They were barred from the "tree of life." Worst of all, they had to leave the constant presence of God. Now, instead of walking and talking with Him intimately, they were reduced to worshiping Him with sacrifices from afar.

God Promised a "Seed"

Satan was delighted. Now he had authority over mankind, whom he hated. Instead of ministering *to* God's creation as he was created to do, he gained authority *over* creation. God cursed him because of this: *"And I will put enmity between you and the woman, and between your seed and her seed; he shall bruise you on the head, and you shall bruise him on the heel"* (Genesis 3:15).

This curse really shook up Satan. The "head" is a symbol of the authority he desired. God promised that a man would be born from the seed of Adam and Eve who would crush Satan and take back the authority he had stolen. The Old Testament reveals how the devil tried in every generation to prevent "the seed of woman" from producing the line of descent that would lead to the one who spelled his doom—Jesus Christ.

Although Satan did not fully understand the promise of the "Seed," he knew enough to begin a campaign to destroy it. First, when he saw that Abel's blood sacrifice was acceptable to God, he incited Cain to kill Abel, thinking that would cut off the Seed.

When Satan heard about God's covenant with Abraham and Abraham's seed, he knew that seed had to be killed. Thinking that Abraham's grandson Jacob might be the promised Seed, Satan stirred up enmity between Jacob and his brother Esau, hoping that Esau would kill Jacob and thus destroy the Seed. Jacob, however, stood up in his newfound image as Israel (one who has prevailed with God and man) and found peace with his brother Esau.

Not knowing who the Seed might be, the deceiver then enticed Pharaoh to order the murder of all male Hebrew babies. This scheme failed also. Two Hebrew parents named Amram and Jochebed stood up in their "image of authority" and concealed their baby boy, saving him from certain death. Their son, Moses, who was actually raised in Pharaoh's own household, became God's chosen deliverer to lead the Israelites out of Egyptian slavery.

In the Promised Land, Satan heard that the Seed was to come through King David, so he attacked David's family line. A wicked woman named Jezebel caused the whole of Israel to follow after the false god Baal. She arranged for her daughter, Athaliah, to marry a prince of the family of David and become the queen of Judah. Athaliah was as evil as Jezebel, and when her husband died, she had her son and all his heirs killed.

Surely now the Seed was destroyed! Satan thought he had won. Ah, but there was still one little grandson, Joash, hidden away by a faithful woman who was married to a priest. At the end of seven years, they brought Joash out, crowned him king, and killed Athaliah. Satan came very close to destroying all of David's seed, but he still failed.

During Israel's captivity in Babylon, the king of Babylon, at the suggestion of a man named Haman (who was inspired by Satan), issued a decree to kill all the Jews in the land. Queen Esther, who was a Jew herself, fasted and prayed for three days, went before the king, exposed Haman's treachery, and saved the lives of her people, the Jews! A Jewish queen of a Babylonian stood in her image of authority and saved her nation.

The Promise Fulfilled

Adam surrendered mankind's God-given authority to Satan, but God promised to restore that authority through Adam's Seed. Throughout the Old Testament, all of Satan's best attempts failed to destroy or prevent the promised Seed. The New Testament tells the celebration story of how that Seed, Jesus Christ, the second Adam, appeared and restored man's stolen authority!

Satan kept trying to destroy the Seed. When Jesus was born, and Satan knew who He was, his efforts became desperate. As with Pharaoh, the devil inspired King Herod to order the killing of all male Jewish children in the Jerusalem region who were two years old and under. A man named Joseph stood up in his authority, obeyed God's voice, and took Mary, his wife, and their baby Son to Egypt, where they lived until Herod died.

Once again Satan failed—the Seed was not destroyed. Whenever men stand in their God-given authority, Satan is defeated. God's purpose can never be thwarted. The day arrived when the Seed came into the open:

> *After being baptized, Jesus came up immediately from the water; and behold, the heavens were opened, and he saw the Spirit of God descending as a dove and lighting on Him, and behold, a voice out of the heavens said, "This is My beloved Son, in whom I am well-pleased"* (Matthew 3:16–17).

Now that Satan knew for sure that Jesus was the Seed, he went after Him with a vengeance. In the wilderness, Satan tempted Jesus by promising to give Him all earthly authority if He would simply worship him instead of God. Jesus refused, of course, knowing that His authority came from heaven, not earth. Jesus already knew who He was as well as the source and nature of the power He possessed. Jesus never disputed Satan's claim of earthly authority; He simply said, *"It is written, 'You shall worship the Lord your God and serve Him only' "* (Luke 4:8).

Since Jesus would not yield to Satan's authority, Satan plotted to kill Him. At first it appeared that Satan had succeeded when Jesus died on the cross, but even that was all part of God's incredible plan! Satan never took Jesus' life; Jesus gave His life willingly. Death could not hold Jesus. Three days later He rose from the dead to complete His Father's plan to redeem (buy back) the souls of people lost in sin and restore their God-given authority on earth. In doing so, He stripped death and the devil of their power:

> *Therefore, since the children share in flesh and blood, He Himself likewise also partook of the same, that through death He might render powerless him who had the power of death, that is, the devil, and might free those who through fear of death were subject to slavery all their lives* (Hebrews 2:14–15).

A Second Adam

The New Testament pictures Jesus as the "second Adam," sent by God to restore man's authority. What does this mean? Paul stated it this way: *"For as through the one man's* [Adam's] *disobedience the many were made sinners, even so through the obedience of the One* [Jesus] *the many will be made righteous"* (Romans 5:19); *"For since by a man came death, by a man also came the resurrection of the dead. For as in Adam all die, so also in Christ all will be made alive"* (1 Corinthians 15:21–22).

Let's examine the evidence. The "second Adam" had to be a man, like the first Adam, but He also had to be without the sin nature. Jesus was born of a virgin through the Holy Spirit; therefore, the sin nature was not transferred to Him. There was no death in Jesus; only the life of God was in Him.

Whereas the first Adam was disobedient to God, the second Adam had to be totally obedient. Jesus did only what the Father told Him, acting in complete harmony with the Father. He was obedient in everything, even to the point of dying on the cross! His obedience made salvation possible for you and me!

The first Adam was weak, falling prey to Satan's temptations. Jesus was strong enough not only to resist Satan, but also to defeat him completely, winning back Adam's lost authority. This was His purpose in coming:

> *For the devil has sinned from the beginning. The Son of God appeared for this purpose, to destroy the works of the devil* (1 John 3:8).

The *"works of the devil"* that Jesus came to destroy are sickness, poverty, death, and sin.

Paralyze the Devil

Sickness does not come from God; it is a work of Satan. Jesus' authority is greater than Satan's, therefore, we can receive healing:

> *Wherever He entered villages, or cities, or countryside, they were laying the sick in the market places, and imploring Him that they might just touch the fringe of His cloak; and as many as touched it were being cured* (Mark 6:56).

Years ago, a staff member told me about her husband's horrendous back problem. I was unable to go and physically lay hands on him, and he was unable to come to church. So I "sent the Word" to him in prayer and claimed this verse: *"He sent His word and healed them, and delivered them from their destructions"* (Psalm 107:20).

Early the next morning, I had to call his wife concerning another matter, and he answered the phone. He said, "The most unusual thing happened to me yesterday. Something clicked in my back while I was working. It went into place and I was healed. I slept like a baby all night." I asked him what time he was healed, and it was the same time I had sent healing to him according to Psalm 107:20. Under God's authority, all things are possible.

Another work of Satan that Jesus destroyed was poverty. The devil seeks to impoverish people, to ruin them, or to put their focus solely on material things. God gives us power to gain wealth, but He expects us to acknowledge Him as its source and to use it for His glory:

> *But you shall remember the* LORD *your God, for it is He who is giving you power to make wealth, that He may confirm His covenant which He swore to your fathers, as it is this day* (Deuteronomy 8:18).

Jesus came to earth and became poor so that we might become rich. He was not poor spiritually, but He was poor in regard to this world's goods. Temporarily, He willingly surrendered the glory that He had with the Father. God gave us a firsthand example of how to prosper. He sowed His only Son and reaped millions of sons! Certainly the greatest wealth of all is the treasure we receive when we become heirs to the kingdom of God!

Jesus also destroyed the power of death. Death came upon all men because of the first Adam's sin. Jesus, the "second Adam," conquered death and took away its sting: *"O death, where is your victory? O death, where is your sting?"* (1 Corinthians 15:55)

> "Under God's authority, all things are possible."

This is one of Jesus' greatest victories. He died and descended into hell to defeat the evil one and to claim everlasting life for all who would believe in and trust Him. He did this so that you and I could have power over death!

Finally, but most importantly, Jesus came to loose us from the hold of sin. Sin has to do with lawlessness, disobedience, error, wickedness, and missing the mark. All of these terms describe our lives away from God. The death and resurrection of Jesus set us free from sin and its hold on us:

> *But now that you have been set free from sin and have become slaves to God, the benefit you reap leads to holiness, and the result is eternal life. For the wages of sin is death, but the gift of God is eternal life in Christ Jesus our Lord* (Romans 6:22–23 NIV).

Restoration of the Lost

Jesus' triumph on the cross restored the four things that Adam and Eve had lost: dominion over the earth, rights to the tree of life, the ability to live in the image of God, and the hope of living forever in a perfect environment like the Garden of Eden. Stop for a moment and meditate on this: Jesus defeated the devil, took authority over the earth, and then gave that authority to you!

Jesus has restored rightful dominion to those for whom it was first intended. All you have to do is believe in Him and He will make it possible for you to do "His" kind of work:

> *Truly, truly, I say to you, he who believes in Me, the works that I do, he will do also; and greater works than these he will do; because I go to the Father* (John 14:12).

Have you ever needed to get a document signed by a person who could not physically be there to sign it? That person can give you the authority to handle legal matters in his name. Such authority is called "the power of attorney." That person has to trust you, however, before he will give you the right to sign in his name! Jesus has given us "power of attorney" to do His work here on earth. He trusts us to represent Him honorably and truthfully.

When Adam and Eve disobeyed God, they were cut off from the tree of life and God stationed cherubim and a flaming sword to guard it. Jesus has restored to us access to that tree—the tree of eternal life. The fruit of the tree of life are righteousness and fulfilled desires. Jesus made us righteous through His sacrifice, and *"the fruit of the righteous is a tree of life"* (Proverbs 11:30). He gives us the desires of our heart, and *"desire fulfilled is a tree of life"* (Proverbs 13:12).

Through Christ, we are fully restored to the image of God. Man was originally made in God's image, but when Adam fell into Satan's trap, he gave up his godly image for an evil one. Now Jesus has cleansed away that evil, so that we can once again reflect the glory of God.

Best of all, Jesus has purchased for us the right to enter a perfect environment. If the Garden of Eden was wonderful, heaven is beyond our wildest dreams! The home which Jesus prepares for us has no curse, no death, no tears, and no pain. Can you imagine this incredible new earth, where God will physically be with us forever? When Jesus comes again to bring a new heaven and a new earth, there will again be an actual tree of life:

> *On either side of the river was the tree of life, bearing twelve kinds of fruit, yielding its fruit every month; and the leaves of the tree were for the healing of the nations* (Revelation 22:2).

Claim Your Inheritance

If you are in a tough spot—between a rock and a hard place—what are you going to do? Claim your position of authority. As a child of God, believe that Jesus has restored your inheritance. You are to rule with Him:

> *I pray that the eyes of your heart may be enlightened, so that you will know what is the hope of His calling, what are the riches of the glory of His inheritance in the saints* (Ephesians 1:18).

Unfortunately, Satan hasn't gotten the message yet. He is still fighting the battle, even though he has already lost the war. If you are not taking authority over Satan, he is taking authority over you. Your physical and spiritual life, your possessions, and your family are all things that Satan would like to steal and destroy, but he has lost his power over you. Jesus has crushed the devil and you are to do the same thing.

"Your inheritance is power and authority over the devil."

Once, I was invited to speak at a large church in Cincinnati, Ohio. I arrived at the airport late at night with a number of boxes containing my tapes and books. As I watched the boxes being removed from the luggage carrier, I noticed someone was heading for the exit with a piece of luggage exactly like mine. I ran after the man and asked him if he had my luggage. When I challenged him, he dropped the bag and ran. He had meant to steal it, but the Holy Spirit directed my attention to him so that my luggage could be recovered. The devil cannot steal from you if you will stand in the authority of Jesus' name!

Your inheritance is power and authority over the devil. God wants you to experience this power! Notice, this power is for those who *believe*. If you are not a born-again believer in Jesus Christ, if you don't believe that you reign with Jesus, if you don't stand in the image of God, it won't work. Get to know the power that you have in Christ, and then use it!

He Is the Head

One of the most common images in the New Testament for the church is that of a body. Jesus is the head and we, His followers, are the body. How do your head and body get along? Your body goes where your head directs! That is exactly what we are to be doing. As the body of Christ, we are called to do as He does:

> *He is also head of the body, the church; and He is the beginning, the first-born from the dead, so that He Himself will come to have first place in everything* (Colossians 1:18).

Jesus is the head, and He intercedes for the body. He sends power to the body. He sends the Holy Spirit to the body. The more we look at Jesus, the more we want to be like Him. The more we trust Him, the more we come to know Him, and the more we know Him, the more we love Him. Our nature changes to become more like His. Just as He intercedes for us in heaven as our great high priest, so also we begin to intercede for others here on earth.

The more we grow in faith and love for the Lord, the more we want to see His Word work in our lives and in the lives of others, and the more we want to see His Spirit move in power. The more we know Him, the more we will delight in Him. Our desires become conformed to His desires, and Psalm 37:4 becomes true in our lives: *"Delight yourself in the LORD; and He will give you the desires of your heart."* As we delight ourselves in the Lord, our desires come into line with Him in whom we are delighting, and we receive not only what we want, but also what He wants!

Some days life just seems too hard. Maybe you have had weeks or even months of discouragement where Satan has tried to draw your attention away from God's plan for your life. That is why it is vitally important for you to claim the authority of Jesus over your world. Don't allow the world to overcome you; you are to overcome the world. Affect the world wherever you go instead of letting the world affect and mold you: *"For whatever is born of God overcomes the world; and this is the victory that has overcome the world—our faith"* (1 John 5:4).

You can overcome the influences and evil of the world because you have the Greater One inside you, and you bear His image. That image is an image of authority!

Your Areas of Authority

Suppose your boss said to you "I am going on a trip; take over while I am gone." You might be thrilled to be "the boss" for a while, but before long you would begin to have questions about your authority: "Can I write checks?" "Can I hire and fire people?" "Should I make important decisions on my own?" Soon you would be calling your boss to find out exactly what authority he had left to you.

Like any good leader, Jesus made it very clear where the believer's authority lies. First, you have authority over the influences of evil men who rule over others. Next, you have authority over principalities, powers, and demonic forces:

> *Behold, I have given you authority to tread upon serpents and scorpions, and over all the power of the enemy, and nothing will injure you* (Luke 10:19).

You also have authority over affliction, sickness, and disease. In all these things you are more than a conqueror because you are supposed to win. You are to take authority over situations:

> *These things speak and exhort and reprove with all authority. Let no one disregard you* (Titus 2:15).

Take authority over bad habits and things that threaten your faith. Let the Holy Spirit show you how:

> *Do you not know that your body is a temple of the Holy Spirit who is in you, whom you have from God, and that you are not your own? For you have been bought with a price: therefore glorify God in your body* (1 Corinthians 6:19–20).

As a nutshell summary, here are seven biblical steps to taking your God-given authority and reigning in victory in your life:

1. You rule through Jesus Christ.—Romans 5:17
2. You live by keeping the Word in your mouth.—Matthew 4:4
3. God crushes Satan under your feet.—Romans 16:20
4. You claim your inheritance of power.—Ephesians 1:17–19
5. You take your seat with Christ in heavenly places.—Ephesians 2:5–7
6. You become a world overcomer.—1 John 4:4

7. You receive your victory in faith.—1 John 5:4

Although authority belongs to you the moment you are born again, you must practice in order to use it effectively. Practice using the Word and taking a stand against the enemy. Satan will fight you. He will not give up an inch of ground without a battle. Submit yourself to God in childlike faith, trusting Him to fight the battle for you. Take Jesus' Word into your circumstances. Claim your inheritance and exercise your authority in Jesus' name and under His rule as head, and you will experience the victory that He desires for you!

STEPS TO A SIMPLER FAITH

1. Think of a time in the last few days when you have given up your authority. What can you do now to reclaim it?
2. Jesus restored things that Adam and Eve lost in the Garden. Choose one of them and explain to a friend how it has been personally restored to you.
3. In your journal or Scripture notebook, write down some biblical examples of your God-given power to "reign in life."
4. Pray for a greater revelation of your authority when using the name of Jesus. List three to five things you should do in that name.
5. Meditate on the verses in Ephesians 6:14–17 and practice putting on the armor of God. Relate to a friend how that armor protects you and how it could protect him or her!

CHAPTER EIGHT

Faith That Gets Prayers Answered

Sometimes, even when we claim our God-given authority, speak the Word, and believe for our victory, nothing happens. Our prayers seem to be unanswered. Why? Is there some secret, some key that unlocks instant and consistent answers to prayer? No. God will not be manipulated. He has, however, promised to answer the prayers of His people. The Bible is full of assurances that God hears our prayers and delights to grant our requests.

Why, then, do we experience times when the answer does not come or is long delayed? There could be many reasons. Perhaps the timing is not right. Spiritual opposition from the enemy can sometimes delay the answer. God may withhold the answer for a while to help us grow stronger in our faith and learn patience, trust, and persistence. Also, prayers uttered from a wrong motive will not be answered.

What are the qualities of faith that gets prayers answered? How can we learn to practice the kind of faith that *always gets what it asks of God*? To begin with, let's return to the example of a child.

As we have already seen, effective faith—faith that gets results—is simple, childlike faith. Imagine a young girl who desires a bicycle and asks her father for one. Her faith is *simplicity* itself. She recognizes a need and asks for that need: "Daddy, can I have a bicycle?"

By turning to her father with her request, she demonstrates *trust* that he can supply her need. Questions of cost or timing or anything else do not trouble her; she just knows her daddy can do it.

If her father does not answer her right away, she continues to ask. This shows *persistence*. Any parent knows how persistent a child can be when asking for something! The girl and her father may be shopping and pass by the bicycle section. "Daddy, can I have a bicycle?" She knows what she wants and will continue to ask until her father answers.

Finally, her father says, "Yes, you may have a bicycle." She may not get it right away—she might have to wait for Christmas or her birthday—but from that moment she displays absolute *confidence* that her request will be granted. Everywhere she goes she says excitedly, "I'm getting a bicycle! I'm getting a bicycle!" When someone asks her, "How do you know you are getting a bicycle?" she replies with certainty, "*Because Daddy said so!*"

During the only trip that He took outside the borders of Israel, Jesus encountered a Gentile woman who demonstrated just this kind of child-like faith. She exhibited simplicity, trust, persistence, and confidence, and in the end, received what she asked.

Before you say, "I could never have that kind of faith," you need to understand that you and I probably would *never* have regarded this woman as a person of great faith. After all, she was a Gentile who likely did not know Jesus very well at all, except by reputation. Being a non-Jew, she was not a member of the "chosen race," and she probably had little or no knowledge of the Scriptures or of anything dealing with God's covenant with His people. Jesus' disciples wanted to get rid of her, and even Jesus Himself *appeared* to treat her rudely at first.

Like so many of us, she had little going for her. All she had was her need and her unwavering belief that Jesus could meet her need. In the end, that was enough. Jesus answered her prayer and called her a woman of *great* faith. Her example proves that if *you* do what *she* did you can get what she got—answered prayer. The key is to never, never give up!

Never, Never, Never Give Up

During World War II, as English cities and towns were being bombed daily, Prime Minister Winston Churchill wanted to encourage the English people. Their homes were being destroyed, their friends and neighbors were dying, and the Nazis appeared to be winning the war. What could Churchill say to his people in these terrible circumstances? He sent one clear message: "Never, never, never give up!"

Often, when times seem the darkest and your prayers are unanswered, you may feel like giving up. Some people might think you are foolish to keep praying and believing when you are not seeing results. They may even blame you for the situation, believing that if you had done things *their* way, everything would be all right. Don't take such criticism to heart. Faith that gets prayers answered is faith that never, never, never gives up!

The Canaanite woman who persistently appealed to Jesus for help is only one of many wonderful examples of passionate faith in the Bible. Hers is an inspiring story of someone who persisted and triumphed against the odds. Even though her situation seemed hopeless, she came to Jesus with faith that would not quit.

> *Jesus went away from there, and withdrew into the district of Tyre and Sidon. And a Canaanite woman from that region came out and began to cry out, saying, "Have mercy on me, Lord, Son of David; my daughter is cruelly demon-possessed." But He did not answer her a word. And His disciples came and implored Him, saying, "Send her away, because she keeps shouting at us"* (Matthew 15:21–23).

This woman's daughter was suffering terribly from demon possession—perhaps wracked by convulsions and delusions as she was being consumed by the devil. When her mother heard that Jesus had come to town, she went out to Him fully trusting that He *could* heal her child.

In these verses, she demonstrated the first two qualities of faith that gets prayers answered:

1. *Simplicity*—She *recognized* her need and *expressed* it openly.

2. *Trust*—She *believed* Jesus could meet her need.

Whenever you get ready to go to God with a request, take time to search your heart. Make sure that you truly believe that He can and will provide.

Because this woman was a Gentile, one of the "accursed" race who had no right to approach Jesus, she called out to Him from a distance: *"Have mercy on me, Lord, Son of David!"* Can you imagine the agony she must have felt over her daughter's condition? Her cry must have been loud, anguished, and heartbreaking. Even so, verse 23 says that Jesus did not even answer her!

Rejected by Jesus?

When I first read this story, I almost could not believe it! How could our gracious and loving Lord have ignored such a desperate cry for help? This woman wasn't even asking for herself, but for her daughter. She was unselfish, respectful, and full of faith. Still, Jesus ignored her! Sometimes we may feel that God treats us the same way. We plead, "Lord, You know how much I need this. I have come to You in complete faith. I am not even asking this for myself. Why aren't You answering me?"

As if being ignored by Jesus wasn't hard enough, His disciples outright rejected her. "Send her away," they said. "She is really annoying us." Have you ever been treated poorly like that by other believers, perhaps even by people in leadership? Have others looked down on you, perhaps told you that your prayers are ineffective, or that you don't have enough faith? Criticism and rejection such as that can make you want to give up.

Imagine God's chosen ministers wanting to be rid of this Canaanite woman! Where was their compassion? Because she did not fit the "profile" of the type of person they thought they were "called" to minister to, they discarded her. Would you give up on God's healing if a pastor or evangelist was abrasive or rude to you concerning your need? This woman didn't! She *knew* why she was there and refused to have her faith denied. Surely she must have felt discouraged by the response she received from Jesus and His disciples, but she never gave up!

What happened next sounds incredible:

> *But He answered and said, "I was sent only to the lost sheep of the house of Israel." But she came and began to bow down before Him, saying, "Lord, help me!" And He answered and said, "It is not good to take the children's bread and throw it to the dogs"* (Matthew 15:24–26).

Jesus said, *"I was sent only to the lost sheep of the house of Israel."* That must have been a real shocker! Healing was for the Jews, but not for the likes of her. Have you ever felt that healing was for a certain select few and that you were not among them? Someone may have even told you that. Notice, however, that this woman did not simply accept rejection and go away angry or defeated, which is exactly what most of us would have done. Instead, she got even closer to Jesus. She knelt before Him, worshiped Him, and asked Him again, *"Lord, help me!"*

Again Jesus appeared to reject her: *"It is not good to take the children's bread and throw it to the dogs."*

Did Jesus actually call this woman a "dog"? How insulting! Dogs are frequently mentioned throughout the Scriptures. The Hebrews used them to guard their houses and flocks. Packs of hungry semi-wild dogs wandered about the fields and streets of the cities, eating garbage and fighting among themselves. Psalm 22, verses 16 and 20, refer to fierce and cruel enemies as "dogs." Because the dog was an unclean animal, people sometimes called themselves "dogs" in acknowledgment of their failings and as a way of humbling themselves.

> "Refuse to have your faith denied."

The more I studied Jesus' words, the more I realized that He was not insulting this woman at all. He knew exactly what He was saying. The "children" were the children of Israel, and their "bread" was Jesus, the Bread of Life. The Jews often called the Gentiles "dogs." Although most Jews rejected Jesus, some Gentiles received Him. Perhaps Jesus' words reflected the attitude that His own disciples had toward this Canaanite woman, and He was trying to show them what was in their hearts.

The Proud Receive Nothing

By her refusal to give up, the Canaanite woman demonstrated the third quality of effective faith and prayer: *persistence*. Boldly, she answered Jesus' challenge:

> *But she said, "Yes, Lord; but even the dogs feed on the crumbs which fall from their masters' table." Then Jesus said to her, "O woman, your faith is great; it shall be done for you as you wish." And her daughter was healed at once* (Matthew 15:27–28).

What simple but powerful faith this woman had! She did not claim any right to the bread of the children; all she asked for was the crumbs! Isn't that amazing? She could have puffed up with pride and said, "I am every bit as good as any Jew!" Instead, she humbled herself. Recognizing and acknowledging her own unworthiness, she would settle for crumbs, knowing that even the crumbs of Jesus' love would be enough!

To be effective in prayer and honest before God, we must come to Him in humility. Which prayer most delights and honors God and brings a positive response from Him: the one that says, "I am a good Christian; I go to church every week and I read my Bible; I am better than most of the people around me, so I expect You to answer my prayer"; or the one that says, "Lord, I can do nothing at all without You; I don't deserve Your love and compassion, but I totally depend on You"? The first is like the proud Pharisee of Luke 18:10–14, whose "prayer" was a personal bragging session that moved God not at all, while the second is like the repentant tax collector in the same story who humbled himself before God and went home a new man.

Have you ever felt that Jesus was not listening when you prayed or that He was refusing to help you? It may have seemed that way to this Canaanite woman, but she refused to leave without her miracle. Jesus' plan for this strange conversation was perfect. His *apparent* harshness brought out her passionate faith. Jesus loved her and was pleased by her persistence. He planned all along to answer her request and heal her daughter. His compassion for her led Him to take the approach He took in order to bring out the boldness and passion in her faith.

Here is the point: Even when you feel like you have been ignored or turned down in prayer, keep asking and keep believing, the way the Canaanite woman did. In the end, you will receive your answer. The Lord will grant your request.

Jesus' trip to the region of Tyre and Sidon—a place He had once compared to Sodom and Gomorrah—was the only time during His earthly life that Jesus left the borders of Israel. I believe He went there solely for the purpose of meeting this woman and satisfying her need. Jesus had been rejected by many of His own people, especially the Jewish religious leaders. He had come as bread for His children, but they did not want to eat. The Bread of Life was "brushed off the table," and when it broke into crumbs, a satisfying portion went to this Gentile woman. He did not insult, ignore, or reject her. On the contrary, He reached out to meet her every need because He loved her and because she never, never, never gave up.

Jesus commended the Canaanite for her "great" faith. Look at the simple childlike quality of it:

- She came to Christ when her situation was hopeless.
- She persisted when her prayer seemed to be denied.
- She still pleaded when obstacles were presented.
- She waited at the feet of the Lord for His mercy.

The timing of Jesus' answers to our prayers can prepare us for victory. Don't walk away when you think that He is rejecting you. Instead, keep on worshiping and trusting Him. Believe passionately that He is going to grant your request. He will.

Don't "Knock" Knocking

One day the disciples asked Jesus to teach them how to pray. He began by giving them the "Lord's Prayer" as a model, then told a parable to nail home the teaching. In the story, a man welcomed an unexpected late-night visitor, but he had no bread to serve his guest. He went to a neighbor's house hoping to borrow three loaves. The neighbor was not happy about being disturbed in the middle of the night. He was already in bed and told his caller that he could not get up to give him anything. Jesus went on to explain:

> *I tell you, although he will not get up and supply him anything because he is his friend, yet because of his shameless persistence and insistence he will get up and give him as much as he needs. So I say to you, Ask and keep on asking and it shall be given you; seek and keep on seeking and you shall find; knock and keep on knocking and the door shall be opened to you. For everyone who asks and keeps on asking receives; and he who seeks and keeps on seeking finds; and to him who knocks and keeps on knocking, the door shall be opened* (Luke 11:8–10 AMP).

On a different occasion, Jesus told another parable that illustrated the same point. A widow seeking legal counsel went to a judge who neither feared nor respected God. Although the judge was unwilling to help her, she continued to plead with him. Finally, he decided to help her, not because he wanted to, but because her persistence was wearing him out! No matter what, she was not going to give up!

Then Jesus brought the point home:

> *And the Lord said, "Hear what the unrighteous judge said; now, will not God bring about justice for His elect who cry to Him day and night, and will He delay long over them? I tell you that He will bring about justice for them quickly. However, when the Son of Man comes, will He find faith on the earth?"* (Luke 18:6–8)

Jesus tells us that we can sometimes get results by simply knocking on the door. At other times, we must be persistent, bringing our request over and over before the throne of God. Unlike the ungodly judge, however, God does not answer us just to get rid of us. God answers us out of love. He answers us because of our persistent faith in who He is—a compassionate and loving God who really cares about our needs. He just loves our consistency when we never, never, never give up.

Blind Faith—Big Benefits

The Gospel of Mark relates the story of a blind man who could have given up before he started, but who instead pressed ahead with persistent faith and received his miracle. Bartimaeus was blind and poor—so poor in fact that he begged daily at the gates of Jericho. The name *Bartimaeus* means "son of a blind man," strongly suggesting that Bartimaeus' father was blind, also. It would have been easy for Bartimaeus to say, "Well, my father was blind his entire life, and I will be too," but he was not about to accept that excuse! When he learned that Jesus of Nazareth was nearby, he jumped at his opportunity:

> *Then they came to Jericho. And as He was leaving Jericho with His disciples and a large crowd, a blind beggar named Bartimaeus, the son of Timaeus, was sitting by the road. When he heard that it was Jesus the Nazarene, he began to cry out and say, "Jesus, Son of David, have mercy on me!" Many were sternly telling him to be quiet, but he kept crying out all the more, "Son of David, have mercy on me!" And Jesus stopped and said, "Call him here." So they called the blind man, saying to him, "Take courage, stand up! He is calling for you." Throwing aside his cloak, he jumped up and came to Jesus. And answering him,*

> *Jesus said, "What do you want Me to do for you?" And the blind man said to Him, "Rabboni, I want to regain my sight!" And Jesus said to him, "Go; your faith has made you well." Immediately he regained his sight and began following Him on the road* (Mark 10:46–52).

Even when the people around him told him to be quiet and not bother Jesus, Bartimaeus refused to be silent. He passionately wanted his eyesight, and he knew Jesus could give it to him.

Bartimaeus received his miracle. His faith demonstrated *simplicity, trust,* and *persistence*—childlike qualities that guaranteed he would get what he asked for. It did not matter if his disease was inherited or if he was as poor as a church mouse. He asked, believed, and never gave up—and received his sight.

This is not the end of the story, however. Regaining his sight changed the direction of Bartimaeus' life. After healing Bartimaeus, Jesus said to him, *"Go; your faith has made you well."* Where did Bartimaeus go? He *"began following* [Jesus] *on the road."* Bartimaeus left behind his familiar surroundings and old way of life and followed Jesus. The Lord is thrilled to answer our prayers when we respond by following Him in all we do and say.

Too often when we have an unanswered prayer we think we have to try harder, show "more" faith, or be a "better" person. This is not so. Neither the Canaanite woman nor blind Bartimaeus tried to earn the "right" to have their prayers answered. They did not say "Hey, Jesus, You have to do this for me because I am so 'good.' "

No, the first thing both of them asked for was *mercy*! In effect they were saying, "Lord, I know I cannot earn this wonderful gift; neither can I pay for it. I have no right even to ask. The only way my prayer can be answered is through Your mercy, Your forgiveness, and Your love." God wants us to acknowledge His Lordship and to humble ourselves before Him. When we do, He pours out His blessings!

Mercy characterizes the essence of our relationship with God! God has always desired a relationship with us, but because of our sinfulness, the only way that such a relationship was possible was for Him to extend His mercy to us.

Our very salvation was achieved by God's mercy for us. Mercy is so essential to salvation that Paul referred to born-again believers as "*vessels of mercy*" (Romans 9:23) and unbelievers as "*vessels of wrath*" (Romans 9:22). Christ's life, death, and resurrection are God's ultimate display of mercy toward us.

"Mercy characterizes the essence of our relationship with God."

When we truly live in Christ, we become so overwhelmed by the gift of God's mercy that we want to share it with everyone—and we become models of His mercy in this world. We also become channels of God's mercy to the world through giving, volunteering, and helping the needy.

Take a moment to ponder the wonder of God's mercy toward you. You did nothing to deserve such a gift. Having received it, your heart should be driven to pass on to others the wonderful gift of God's love and mercy in Christ.

Take a Prayer Inventory

The Bible assures us that God hears our prayers even when it seems that we are not getting any results. Simplicity, trust, and persistence are keys to answered prayer. If you still are seeing no results, it may be time for self-examination. Thoughtfully and prayerfully ask yourself the following questions:

1. "Am I walking in love toward my brothers and sisters and the world around me?" Faith works by love. If your faith isn't working, check your "love level." Remember, Paul told us that it is not our actions that get results, but our love: "*For in Christ Jesus neither circumcision nor uncircumcision means anything, but faith working through love*" (Galatians 5:6).
2. "Are my words to and about others always loving?" Check your conversation as well as your prayers. Are your prayers just about you and what you want, or are you praying in love for those around you? Take a special look at how you treat your family and friends. Sometimes we put great effort into helping strangers and forget to treat those closest to us with love and mercy.
3. "Am I harboring unforgiveness in my heart?" Jesus said, "*Whenever you stand praying, forgive, if you have anything*

against anyone, so that your Father who is in heaven will also forgive you your transgressions" (Mark 11:25). Unforgiveness in your heart will hinder your faith. If you truly want to know why your faith is not working, ask God to expose any remnants of unforgiveness.

4. "Am I harboring any jealousy or strife in my heart?" Do you resent someone who has more wealth or success than you do? Are you competing with someone in your family, church, or workplace? Approach this question prayerfully, for often we cannot see our own envy and selfish ambition. Faith cannot flourish in an atmosphere of jealousy or rivalry. Root them out!

5. "Am I living or operating in fear?" Remember, fear is the enemy of faith. Actions that are fear-driven will bind your faith and prevent you from getting the results you desire. If you are really trusting God, you have nothing to fear. Fear is *not* from God; take authority over it: *"For God has not given us a spirit of timidity, but of power and love and discipline"* (2 Timothy 1:7).

6. "Am I focused on my harvest?" If you want to *grow* beans, you have to *plant* beans. Check your "farming methods." If you desire to harvest souls for the Lord, have you planted the Word in their hearts? If you need help with finances, have you given to others so that you might receive? Are you lonely and need friendship? Have you been a friend to others? Sometimes we have a crop failure because we didn't plant anything! The God-kind of faith is a working faith that plants as well as reaps.

7. "Am I praying from right motives?" Sometimes the motives behind our requests are not really based on faith, but on fleshly desire. We want something because it appeals to us, so we ask the Lord for it. This will not work. As James says, *"You ask and do not receive, because you ask with wrong motives, so that you may spend it on your pleasures"* (James 4:3). When you pray with a wrong motive or selfish purpose, God will not answer your prayer. On the other hand, when you ask according to God's

will, you can proceed with the utmost confidence and expectation. Be honest with yourself and check your motive!

8. "Do I doubt that God hears and will answer my prayer?" When you bring your request to God, believe that He will answer you while you are praying! Drop your doubts; don't let them get in the way of your faith: *"But he must ask in faith without any doubting, for the one who doubts is like the surf of the sea, driven and tossed by the wind. For that man ought not to expect that he will receive anything from the Lord"* (James 1:6–7); *"Therefore I say to you, all things for which you pray and ask, believe that you have received them, and they will be granted you"* (Mark 11:24).

A member of my Bible study group a few years back had had a hip bone removed. The constant pain in her back due to the missing bone made it so that she had to stand all the time.

One day I taught on healing and really made her angry. She said, "Doctors are for healing, Jesus is for your sins, and the two shall never meet." I showed her many, many Scriptures that said Jesus Himself took our infirmities and our diseases, but that just made her more upset.

A few weeks later, a friend invited this woman to a miracle service. The pastor came down into the audience and said, "There are people here with severe back problems. If you will stand up, God is healing back problems right now." This friend urged the woman to stand up, and finally, she did. Immediately, she felt a warmth flow all over her body. Later that evening as she was getting ready for bed, her daughter came into her room and said, "Mother, what is that on your hip? It looks like a hip bone!" God had created a new hip bone—and her back pain was gone forever!

God will help you with your doubts. Just take that first step. Stand up in faith, and ask Him to remove the doubts and replace them with unwavering faith.

9. "Am I substituting emotion for faith?" This is easy to do. When we hear the testimonies of others, our faith can get a spiritual lift. We soar to the mountaintop because someone else's experience has encouraged us. Testimonies of healings and miracles should reinforce our belief in God's Word and

remind us of His faithfulness to fulfill it. Testimonies *are* meant to encourage us, but they can never take the place of digging into God's Word and getting His promise for our situation *firsthand.* Testimonies of healings and miracles should drive you back to the Word, the source of your faith. Make sure you are asking with faith, not emotion. Be joyful over what God has done for others. Praise Him for His wonderful works. Say to yourself, "If God did it for them, He will do it for me!" Then get into the Word for your own sustenance, blessing, and faith-building.

Are you ready to give up? Is the answer to your prayer taking longer than you had hoped? If you have examined your heart according to the questions above; if you are learning to practice simplicity, trust, and persistence and know that you are praying "right," then keep trusting the Lord. God is never late, but He often seems to be last minute! Your answer may not come right away, but it is definitely on its way! Waiting on the Lord is a healthy spiritual discipline: *"Wait for the LORD; be strong and let your heart take courage; yes, wait for the LORD"* (Psalm 27:14). Put your trust in God's timing. It is always perfect.

Have You Checked the Plans?

A builder doesn't just "slap" together a house. Before he lifts a bit of lumber, he checks the blueprints, then rechecks them many times during construction. He knows that if he fails to follow the plans, the house will be a failure. In the same way, you need to check and recheck God's plan for your life.

One time the Lord spoke to me and said, "You should believe for more miracles when you teach." I said, "Lord, You called me to be a teacher; You didn't call me to move in miracles. I don't see in the Bible where teachers move in miracles."

God pulled me up short and reminded me of the time when Nicodemus came to Jesus by night, and said to Him, *"Rabbi, we know that You have come from God as a teacher; for no one can do these signs that You do unless God is with him"* (John 3:2). The Lord showed me that it was not enough to teach the Word; I must also believe for the miraculous. The more I believe for miracles, the more miracles God performs.

Do you know what God's specific call on your life is? Obey that call, and get your faith in line with it. Go back to the Word again and again to be sure you are building your life according to God's blueprint. If He has called you to work with youth on Saturday nights, then don't pray for a job that conflicts with that. God is able to give you a job that leaves you free to do His work. He wants your life to harmonize with His will, and He will not answer prayers that are inconsistent with His plan for your life.

If you are uncertain of the nature of God's call on your life, then go to His Word and pray, asking for His guidance and direction. He wants you to know His will and He will reveal it to you if you sincerely seek. James said, *"But if any of you lacks wisdom, let him ask of God, who gives to all generously and without reproach, and it will be given to him"* (James 1:5).

Sometimes God will answer your prayers instantly. At other times you will need to be persistent. Ask, seek, knock, and keep on asking, seeking, and knocking until you have God's answer to your situation. You may be puzzled about why others get answers while you are still waiting. Check your heart, including your motives and your love walk, and look for any traces of leftover fear or strife. Make sure there are no roadblocks that you have put up which prevent God from answering your prayers. When God shows you areas in your life that need to be changed, *change them.* Be repentant and obedient. No matter what may have happened in the past—no matter which person, teacher, or system may have failed you—God has never failed you and He never will. You can trust Him completely. Childlike faith is simple, trusting, and persistent faith. Persistent faith is passionate faith, and passionate faith pleases God and gets results!

STEPS TO A SIMPLER FAITH

1. Remember three times in your life when faith resulted in blessings. Record them in your journal.
2. Meditate on obstacles to your faith such as fear, envy, doubt, or wrong motives. Ask God to show you through His Word how to combat them.
3. Write down your most urgent or important prayer request. Now list the seeds that you have planted in preparation for your "harvest."

4. For three days, write down every word of doubt that comes out of your mouth. Then take that piece of paper and throw those doubting words in the trash!
5. Find an example in the Scriptures of each of the following:
    - Someone who waited a long time for an answer to prayer.
    - Someone who ignored the rejection and insults of others to pursue his or her godly desire.
    - Someone whose specific request was not fulfilled because God had a better answer.

CHAPTER NINE

Real People, Real Faith

Faith is not a trinket on a shelf that we take out and dust off when we need it. Faith is more like a muscle that has to be exercised daily to keep it strong and supple. Do you have "good" faith days and "bad" faith days—some days when you feel as though you can take on the whole world, and other days when you just want to curl up in a hole somewhere and hide? You *can* stay strong and active in your faith, whether you need atoning faith, life-giving faith, persevering faith, delivering faith, or creative faith.

Maintaining active faith is not always easy, but Hebrews chapter 11 proves it is possible. In this wonderful chapter, the great heroes of faith from the Old Testament are paraded before us for our review. These people encourage us not only by their faith but also because they were so *ordinary*! Essentially, they were no different from you or me. If God could use ordinary people like them, He can use ordinary people like us.

All of these faith heroes failed the Lord at one time or another. Some had blatant and significant areas of weakness that caused trouble for them. Most of them made many mistakes along the way, yet they still trusted God. Because of their faith and in spite of their flaws, God accomplished tremendous things through them.

The writer of Hebrews addressed his letter specifically to a Jewish audience, people who, like many of us, had difficulty believing in what they could not see. Chapter 11 of Hebrews reviews the faith of great men and women in Hebrew history to demonstrate to Jewish believers in Christ that the faith God required of them was nothing new. It was the same faith that had motivated the Hebrew race from the time of Abraham.

This chapter wonderfully illustrates the nature and diverse purposes and functions of faith as well as its power to transform lives:

> *Now faith is the assurance of things hoped for, the conviction of things not seen. For by it the men of old gained approval. By faith we understand that the worlds were prepared by the word of God, so that what is seen was not made out of things which are visible. By faith Abel offered to God a better sacrifice than Cain, through which he obtained the testimony that he was righteous, God testifying about his gifts, and through faith, though he is dead, he still speaks* (Hebrews 11:1–4).

These four verses reveal four specific truths about faith:

- Faith is certain about things it cannot see (verse 1).
- Faith is honorable (verse 2).
- Faith governs our perception of the universe (verse 3).
- Faith wins acceptance and reward from God (verse 4).

As you read these testimonies, consider the wonder and power of faith.

Atonement: Your Way or His Way?

Abel, the first man of faith listed in Hebrews 11, was looking for atonement (reconciliation with God). We all need forgiveness. Even though we know that Jesus has washed away all of our sins, we need to go to Him to acknowledge our weaknesses, confess our sin, and claim His forgiveness.

Prior to the coming of Christ, the Jews and most others offered blood sacrifices on the altar in order to obtain forgiveness. This was a practice that dated back to the days of Abel. In fact, the very first sacrifices recorded in the Bible were those of Cain and Abel. God accepted Abel's offering but rejected Cain's (see Genesis 4:3–5).

Abel recognized that he was sinful and understood that the true way of atonement was to offer a blood sacrifice. He did not try to invent his own path to forgiveness, but followed God's path, demonstrating that he had no righteousness of his own. Knowing that without the shedding of blood there is no remission of sin, Abel threw himself on the mercy of God and was cleansed.

Cain, on the other hand, was probably singing that famous old song, "I Did It My Way," as he came to the altar with the fruit of his hands. Although he brought a thank offering, Cain apparently displayed no recognition of his sin or of his need for atonement. He may have known that a blood sacrifice was called for, but he did not put his faith into action. Even Cain's offering was a gesture of rebellion.

"Faith obeys God's Word."

Abel showed that faith does it God's way! He brought of the firstlings of his flock while Cain brought produce of the cursed ground and his own efforts. Atonement must be freely given by God through the death of an innocent; it cannot be earned by human effort. That is why Abel's offering was accepted and Cain's was not.

Faith obeys God's Word. When you say that you believe (have faith) that your sins are washed away, are you speaking out of pride? Are you harboring the thought that those sins were washed away because you are better than other people? Do you try to wash away your sins by doing "good works," going to church more often, or out-performing your neighbors?

Beware of offering a Cain sacrifice! Your faith for atonement must recognize that only God can wash away your sins. You must sacrifice any pride and turn your sins over to God.

Cain made another mistake: He was religious but not faithful. He wanted to offer a bloodless sacrifice. He went through the motions, but his heart was not in it. How often do you "go through the motions" of reading your Bible, attending church, or reciting prayers? None of these actions can nourish you unless your heart is filled with faith:

> *And without faith it is impossible to please Him, for he who comes to God must believe that He is and that He is a rewarder of those who seek Him* (Hebrews 11:6).

In faith you must actively and constantly focus on God and His salvation. He is not as interested in your actions as He is in your heart. Reach out to Him in faith, and His love will fill your heart and your life.

The Man Who Never Died

The next man of faith mentioned in Hebrews 11 is Enoch, the man who never died:

> *By faith Enoch was taken up so that he would not see death; and he was not found because God took him up; for he obtained the witness that before his being taken up he was pleasing to God. And without faith it is impossible to please Him, for he who comes to God must believe that He is and that He is a rewarder of those who seek Him* (Hebrews 11:5–6).

In the genealogy listed in Genesis 5, we find a monotonous litany of births and deaths. At verse 21, however, we encounter a notable exception:

> *Enoch lived sixty-five years, and became the father of Methuselah. Then Enoch walked with God three hundred years after he became the father of Methuselah, and he had other sons and daughters. So all the days of Enoch were three hundred and sixty-five years. Enoch walked with God; and he was not, for God took him* (Genesis 5:21–24).

Enoch, the seventh generation from Adam, was translated (taken to heaven) without seeing death. The Bible records less than a hundred words about him, yet they are powerful words. Enoch was one of two men who the Bible says "*walked with God.*" No fault is mentioned concerning him. Outside of Jesus, Enoch is the only person of whom it is written, "He pleased God," and he is one of only two who missed death! (The other was Elijah.)

Enoch and Elijah actually have much in common:

- Both were taken to heaven bodily without dying.
- Both were prophets of judgment.
- Both fought idolatry.

Many believe that Enoch and Elijah are the two witnesses mentioned in Revelation 11, who will come to earth to complete their lives and die.

According to the New Testament writer Jude, the days of Enoch were flagrantly wicked, but he preached righteousness and even prophesied Christ's Second Coming:

> *It was also about these men that Enoch, in the seventh generation from Adam, prophesied, saying, "Behold, the Lord came with many thousands of His holy ones, to execute judgment upon all, and to convict all the ungodly of all their ungodly deeds which they have done in an ungodly way, and of all the harsh things which ungodly sinners have spoken against Him"* (Jude 1:14–15).

While others were just living, Enoch walked with God. His walk shows that he agreed with God, for *"Can two walk together, except they be agreed?"* (Amos 3:3 KJV) Enoch pleased God through his faith, for *"without faith it is impossible to please Him."*

Enoch walked with God for 300 years. Genesis 5:22 suggests that he did not start walking with God until he was sixty-five, after the birth of Methuselah, his first son. The name *Methuselah* means, "when this child dies the deluge shall come." Methuselah lived the longest of all men because God in His great mercy did not want to send the deluge (flood). The year Methuselah died, the great flood came.

Growing faith takes you into growing steps of blessing. Enoch went from faith to faith. After 300 years of daily walking in faith with God, he reached the apex of this faith—translation. He never tasted death! Enoch enjoyed a continuous fellowship with God. Nothing, not even death, interrupted that friendship. This pleasing walk of faith is available to you, too! Although there is little likelihood that you will be translated as Enoch was, the warm fellowship he enjoyed with God can be yours as well if you are willing to pursue it.

The Faith That Saved the Human Race

Noah, the next Old Testament hero of faith, also lived in a wicked generation and found grace in the eyes of the Lord:

> *By faith Noah, being warned by God about things not yet seen, in reverence prepared an ark for the salvation of his household, by which he condemned the world, and became an heir of the righteousness which is according to faith* (Hebrews 11:7).

The foundation of Noah's faith was God's Word—he was *"warned by God."* Noah took God's word as truth, even though he had no physical proof that the flood was actually going to happen. He simply believed in *"things not yet seen"* because God had told him of them.

Can you imagine building a huge boat in your backyard? What would the neighbors say? Maybe the newspapers and TV stations would come over to do a report on this crazy person! Perhaps your best friend would try to get you to see a psychiatrist! It must have taken very strong faith for Noah to withstand the ridicule that came from all sides.

Noah had simple, childlike faith. He simply believed God and followed His word even when it meant doing something that looked foolish to others. He remained faithful in spite of what his eyes and ears told him. Acting on the word of an invisible God, Noah spent one hundred years building a boat of enormous dimensions five hundred miles from the nearest body of water, and then filled it with animals. He obeyed God because he believed that God was telling him the truth when He warned of a great flood of judgment coming upon the earth. Noah had no visible signs of the flood until after he was locked inside the ark.

Noah's faith led him to action—he *"prepared an ark"*—and this action served as a witness to his faith *"by which he condemned the world."* Best of all, God rewarded Noah's faith in three wondrous ways: his family was saved, he became an heir of righteousness, and he was given a visible sign of God's faithfulness—the rainbow. (See Genesis 6–9.) Because of his faith, Noah and his entire family were saved from the destruction that fell on the rest of mankind.

Can your faith overcome the ridicule of the world and deliver those you love from destruction? Yes, it can. I know because I saw it happen in my own family. Shortly after I was married, my father had a nervous breakdown. My mother accompanied my husband and me to Dallas for a healing convention. One night, the evangelist called my mother out of the thousands of people present. He said, "You are weeping not for yourself, but for your husband, who has had a nervous breakdown. Take the handkerchief in which you have shed your tears, place it on his body, and he will be healed."

Some people might have said, "What can a used handkerchief do for a man who has had a nervous breakdown?" Surely this was as foolish as building an ark in the middle of a desert! My mother wasn't about to let thoughts like that get in her way! In faith, she took the handkerchief and followed the Lord's instructions. My father began to recover. He did not get well overnight, but day by day he improved.

Our heavenly Father has promised us that we will always have His loving kindness and mercy. When we became born-again believers, we became vessels to extend God's mercy and love to others, including our loved ones. We must reach forth, in faith, to touch and minister to those we love. With our hearts securely grounded in faith, we will know how to meet the needs of others.

"We must reach forth, in faith, to touch and minister to those we love."

Acting on the Word of God delivers us from His judgment! No matter what is happening to the world around you, or what *will* happen, God is able to provide a way of escape, a place of safety! Have faith in God!

Eyes on the Eternal

Another hero who put his faith into action was Abraham. Originally named *Abram*, which means "father of altitude," he received his new name, *Abraham*, which means "father of a multitude," from God a year before Isaac was born.

> *By faith Abraham, when he was called, obeyed by going out to a place which he was to receive for an inheritance; and he went out, not knowing where he was going. By faith he lived as an alien in the land of promise, as in a foreign land, dwelling in tents with Isaac and Jacob, fellow heirs of the same promise; for he was looking for the city which has foundations, whose architect and builder is God* (Hebrews 11:8–10).

Here was a man who followed God obediently without knowing where he was going. With simple trust, Abraham answered God's call on his life and followed His directions to a new land, always ready to move whenever God called. He focused his eyes not on his earthly inheritance, which was enormous, but on heavenly things. He was looking toward his permanent dwelling place. Abraham's example reveals that living in the altitude of God's Word brings a multitude of results.

Abraham's wife Sarah was a woman of faith. God promised that she would be the "mother of nations" (see Genesis 17:16), and she believed Him, even when it looked at times as though that promise would never be fulfilled. Sarah was childless and well past menopause, and Abraham was even older. Nevertheless, they both deeply desired to have a child.

> *By faith even Sarah herself received ability to conceive, even beyond the proper time of life, since she considered Him faithful who had promised. Therefore there was born even of one man, and him as good as dead at that, as many descendants as the stars of heaven in number, and innumerable as the sand which is by the seashore* (Hebrews 11:11–12).

What kind of faith would it take to believe that God would provide a baby in their circumstances? Through her faith, Sarah received miracle-working power that quickened her body as well as Abraham's. This ninety-year-old woman gave birth to a child who would become a patriarch of Israel. In faith, Sarah kept her eyes on God and trusted in His promises.

Several years ago a couple came to me in despair. Doctors had told them they could not have a child. I went out with them for coffee after a service one night, and I shared how God had miraculously given us a natural child. Doctors had told me the same thing: "You can never have a child." This couple said, "Would you agree in prayer for us?" So we agreed in prayer, right there in the coffee shop. They moved away shortly after that, and I lost track of them for a while. Imagine my joy when they dropped by to show me a beautiful baby boy! Through faith, we receive healing and life!

Following God in faith can be hard. Our faith can be tested in many ways at many times, but Abraham faced one of the most terrible tests of all and passed with flying colors! He won the gold medal of faith:

> *By faith Abraham, when he was tested, offered up Isaac, and he who had received the promises was offering up his only begotten son; it was he to whom it was said, "In Isaac your descendants shall be called." He considered that God is able to raise people even from the dead, from which he also received him back as a type* (Hebrews 11:17–19).

God asked him to sacrifice Isaac—the son of promise—as a burnt offering. Abraham had such unquestioning faith in God's Word that he quietly did what God required, not understanding why but knowing that somehow God would raise Isaac from the dead. Of course, God stopped Abraham from actually killing Isaac and provided a ram for Abraham to sacrifice instead. By his actions, Abraham proved his faith and trust in God and earned his title, "father of faith" (see Genesis 22:1–18).

In type and symbolism all this—offering up Isaac, receiving him back as if from the dead, and a substitutionary sacrifice (the ram)—looked ahead to the time of Christ. Jesus, the only begotten Son of God, died on a cross as a substitutionary sacrifice for our sins. Through the resurrection, the Father received His Son back from the dead.

When you receive difficult commands from the Lord, it is a blessing to obey even when you don't understand the "why" of the instruction. Many of God's greatest blessings are lost when we say "no" to the Lord because we are unwilling to take a risk. Abraham was willing to give up one son, and his descendants became as the sands of the sea. He was given back his son along with countless more descendants. Obedience to God brings a sure and abundant return every time!

Faith Makes Hard Choices

Try to imagine being a Hebrew slave in Egypt, expecting a child, and suddenly Pharaoh has ordered all newborn boys to be killed. When your baby is born, he is the most beautiful little boy you have ever seen! What would you do? Would you be terrified of Pharaoh's power and submit to his decree, or would you defy his order because you have a higher allegiance?

This actually was the situation faced by Moses' parents, Amram and Jochebed. Because of their strong faith in the Lord, they did not fear Pharaoh's decree:

> *By faith Moses, when he was born, was hidden for three months by his parents, because they saw he was a beautiful child; and they were not afraid of the king's edict* (Hebrews 11:23).

Amram and Jochebed must have heard from God because faith like theirs can come only from hearing the Word of God. *Amram* means "the people exalted." His son was to be part of a divine plan that would exalt his people. *Jochebed* means "Jehovah is glorious." She glorified God with her active faith. These parents saw only slavery and evil coming from their earthly ruler, but they looked beyond that to God, and they knew that He was in control.

Their faith gave them the strength to put their tiny baby into a basket and float him down the river. They knew in their hearts that God had a plan, and they turned their baby over to His care. As parents, we can fret and worry over our children, or we can turn them over to God, who loves them even more than we do.

Hebrews chapter 11 devotes more space to Moses than to any other individual. His life was marked by crises. The child of Hebrew slaves in Egypt, Moses nevertheless was rescued from his little basket in the river by the daughter of Pharaoh, who raised him as her own. Because he grew up in the king's house, Moses was trained for leadership and received a high-class education. Had things been different, he might even have become pharaoh one day. Isn't it interesting that the pharaoh who desired to keep Israel permanently enslaved would give food, lodging, and education to the very man who would bring about Israel's freedom? (See Exodus 2:1–10.)

In spite of all the earthly privileges he enjoyed in Pharaoh's house, Moses refused to be called the son of Pharaoh's daughter. Instead, he chose to identify with his own people. He knew that God had called him to deliver his people from slavery, and he would rather be a godly slave than a heathen king. He would rather suffer with the people of God than to enjoy the pleasures of sin. Despite the wealth, power, and authority that were his in Pharaoh's household, Moses resolutely refused them!

> *By faith Moses, when he had grown up, refused to be called the son of Pharaoh's daughter, choosing rather to endure ill-treatment with the people of God than to enjoy the passing pleasures of sin, considering the reproach of Christ greater riches than the treasures of Egypt; for he was looking to the reward* (Hebrews 11:24–26).

Moses received a revelation of the coming Messiah. He knew that suffering with Him, whatever the cost, was a greater treasure than all the riches of Egypt. For Moses, the unseen reward of obeying the voice of God was more desirable than all the wealth of Egypt.

In Christ there are true treasures that cannot be compared with any glitter the world might offer. Respect God's reward: It will help you to live the faith life diligently. Look to Him, not men. That will keep your faith alive and never disappointed! Keep your eyes on God's goals.

Faith Crosses the Waters

Moses eventually led the Hebrews out of Egypt. They left a place of slavery and poverty, just as we escaped the slavery and poverty of Satan's world when we accepted Jesus as our Savior and Lord.

Like us, the Israelites were under a new Lord, but the old one did not give up easily. Pharaoh fought long and hard to keep the Israelites, but finally, after ten increasingly dire plagues on his land and people, he let them go. Angry over their departure, angry over the deaths of their firstborn, including his own, and angry over losing a free labor force, Pharaoh change his mind and determined to bring the Hebrews back or destroy them in the process.

Like Pharaoh, Satan seldom gives up his slaves of sin without a fight. Moses encouraged the people to move on in faith, and God rewarded them. He opened the Red Sea and they crossed over to safety from their enemies! They were in a hard place—the sea before them, the Egyptian army behind them—but they stepped out in faith. They crossed over the sea on dry ground, but the pursuing Egyptians drowned to the last man.

God has creative ways of getting us over seemingly impossible obstacles! (See Exodus 14:15–18.) Pharaoh was sure he had won. His former slaves were trapped between the Red Sea and the biggest army in the world. They would never get away! How could he have ever imagined that big sea dividing to reveal a way of escape? Who could have anticipated that Moses would have enough faith to stay calm in the face of sure destruction, and reach out his arm in faith?

God can use our faith to open paths where every way seems closed off. Once, the Lord told me to pass out Bibles to Jewish people. I soon discovered, however, that Israeli law forbids the distribution of Bibles in that country. Still, my faith was strong that God wanted me to proceed with this plan. God is so creative in overcoming obstacles. At that time 30,000 Jewish soldiers were stationed in Lebanon. The Lord told me, "Cross the border. Lebanon has no such laws." We crossed the border and passed out Bibles to all those soldiers! It was such a blessing to watch young Israeli soldiers sitting on their tanks and reading the New Testament!

When you face obstacles so big that you see no way around them, just remember that God has prepared a miracle. Reach out in faith, and He will carry you across *"and nothing will be impossible to you"* (Matthew 17:20).

"God has creative ways of getting us over seemingly impossible obstacles!"

Once you accepted the salvation of Jesus, you angered Satan! Just like Pharaoh, Satan is angry that you have left his sinful traps behind and angry that he has lost control of your behavior. He will come after you and push you to your limits, hoping to recapture you. When this happens, remember Moses and the Israelites! If you are trapped between Satan's army and the Red Sea, step out in faith. God will certainly deliver you and richly reward you. The Lord is just as much *your* deliverer as He was Moses' deliverer!

You Can Be a Faith Hero, Too!

No matter how small and weak you may feel, your faith and walk with God *can* please Him. He wants to have continuous, unbroken fellowship with His children. Like Enoch, you can agree with God and spend your lifetime walking in harmony with Him. Doing things God's way, even when you don't understand it, always brings a blessing.

Faith delivered Noah and his whole household during an age when the rest of the world was in rebellion against God. Through faith, Noah survived ridicule and overcame doubt. He trusted God's Word even when his eyes and ears gave him different messages. His reward was the saving of his family from destruction and an everlasting promise from God.

God called Abraham to walk away from his actual family to become the patriarch of an intangible one. In faith he followed God's voice, and he was rewarded with riches in this life. Abraham proved his faith and trust in God when he dared to obey God and offered his son as a sacrifice. He learned during his faith walk that God is true to His Word.

Moses' parents were full of faith to believe that God had a future for their son who was condemned by Pharaoh to die. No matter how hopeless it may seem for your son or daughter, have faith that God can redeem your present circumstances and turn them around for a blessing. Moses learned to know His God step by step as he followed Him in obedience.

He did not have the written Word as we do; he had to listen daily to God's voice, and be obedient. That was the greatest qualification for an effective leader in those days, and it still is today! Remember, *"Faith comes from hearing, and hearing by the word of Christ"* (Romans 10:17).

This brief review of great men and women of faith should make it clear that God gives faith for every situation in every age. Some received faith to do the impossible, others to endure ridicule, and some to give up earthly pleasures—but they were all rewarded for their faith!

God is the source of your faith. His kind of faith will cover every circumstance you will ever face. He will never call you to a place or a work without equipping you fully to be successful. God will meet you where you are with His kind of faith. Receive His faith and be a vessel for His use. Your faith will increase and become strong only as you exercise it. Follow the example of these faith heroes from Hebrews chapter 11. Put your faith into action!

STEPS TO A SIMPLER FAITH

1. Record two events in your journal where your faith delivered you from Satan's trap.
2. You can be a leader like Moses. Each one of us is a leader in some capacity. You may be the leader at your job, in your neighborhood, at your church, or in your family. Study the leadership qualities discussed in 1 Timothy 3 and 4. List as many as you can. Then pray and ask God to develop you in the leadership area that He has for you.
3. Find and meditate on a Scripture for each of these kinds of faith:
    - Atoning Faith
    - Life-giving Faith
    - Persevering Faith
    - Delivering Faith
    - Creative Faith
4. Has God ever asked you to do a difficult thing? Share your situation and response with a friend or mentor today.

5. Meditate on Matthew 17:20. How will this help you put feet to your faith? Record your thoughts in your journal or Scripture notebook.

CHAPTER TEN

You Have Friends in High Places

Have you ever been lonely or just needed someone to talk to, someone who understands you and accepts you just the way you are? That is what a friend does. *True* friends are a rare commodity in this world. Like most of us, you probably have many casual acquaintances, but how many people in your life do you regard as a true friend with whom you can share your deepest thoughts and most intimate feelings?

Friendships grow as acquaintances begin to spend time together, getting to know one another, discovering common interests, and learning each other's likes and dislikes and beliefs and values. It is extremely difficult, if not impossible, for two people to develop a true and strong friendship from a distance or if they rarely spend time with each other. Is there anyone in your life with whom you share this kind of relationship? If so, count yourself truly blessed.

As important as human friendship is, even more important is friendship with God. You may know God as your Father, your King, your Savior and Lord, and the source of all blessings, but do you know Him as your friend? Perhaps you have never thought of the Lord that way or feel that the idea of friendship with Him is too good to be true. It isn't! God wants to spend time with you; He desires to walk with you and hear about your troubles, your trying times, and your happy moments. He wants to talk with you all the time. God longs to fellowship with you on every level. With a friend like Him, you need never be lonely again.

Is friendship with God truly possible? Yes. James 2:23 refers to Abraham as the *"friend of God."* Exodus 33:11 says, *"The Lord used to speak to Moses face to face, just as a man speaks to his friend."* Jesus made it absolutely clear that friendship with us is what He has in mind:

> *Greater love has no one than this, that one lay down his life for his friends. You are My friends if you do what I command you. No longer do I call you slaves, for the slave does not know what his master is doing; but I have called you friends, for all things that I have heard from My Father I have made known to you* (John 15:13–15).

These verses occur in the context of the importance of our abiding in Christ. Friendship with the Lord means spending enough time with Him to get to know Him intimately, as He already knows us. It means being in fellowship with Him.

"Jesus is the best friend you will ever have."

It is the Lord who calls us into fellowship with Himself, not the other way around. We usually feel as though we are calling upon Him, but we call on Him because He first called us.

One morning I was praying at our kitchen table and telling the Lord what a privilege it was to live for Him. He spoke to me and said, "You don't live *for Me*, you live *with Me*. We live together and are seated together in heavenly places. When you pray, we come together in fellowship."

Isn't that wonderful? When we know the Lord we are never alone because He is Jehovah-Shammah—the God who is present. He has promised never to leave us or forsake us (see Hebrews 13:5). Instead, He desires us to enter into continual, unbroken fellowship with Him.

Jesus is the best friend you will ever have. If you take a walk with Him every day, just the two of you, very soon you will find your faith growing strong and your blessings multiplying.

You Are in Good Company

Enoch knew all about fellowship with God. Remember, Enoch is the man who *"walked with God"* for 300 years and then *"was not, for God took him"* (Genesis 5:22, 24). For Enoch, friendship with God was more important than anything else. He enjoyed such intimate fellowship with God that the day came when God took him to heaven. As someone once put it, Enoch and God were walking together one day and spent the day deep in conversation. Toward the end of the day, God said, "Enoch, it's getting late and My house is closer than yours; why don't you come home with Me?"

A few generations later Noah, a descendant of Enoch, also walked with God in spite of the fact that all the rest of mankind was going in another direction. Noah maintained such close fellowship with God that God shared His plans with him. He told Noah how disappointed He was in man and how He planned to destroy all mankind with a flood.

Noah trusted God's Word. Years of close fellowship had taught him to listen to the Lord. When God instructed him to build an ark to save his entire household from destruction, Noah did not hesitate to obey. His intimate fellowship with God had built strong faith in him so that he believed God without question. The reward he received for his faithfulness was life for himself and his family.

Enoch and Noah are the only people whom the Bible says *"walked with God."* The Hebrew word for "walk" is *halak*, which means "to walk up and down, to be conversant." Later, the Bible describes Moses as walking and talking with God in much the same way that Adam did.

An Honest Relationship

Moses' desire to know God was so great that he is one of only two people in the Old Testament (Abraham is the other) who is described specifically as God's "friend." As Exodus 33:11 indicates, Moses had a "face-to-face" relationship with God. They were on intimate speaking terms. Moses loved God, worshiped God, and revered God—and even got upset with God from time to time!

One of the characteristics of true friendship is honesty. When God first called Moses to lead His people out of Egypt, Moses didn't want the job. He said, *"O Lord, please send someone else to do it"* (Exodus 4:13 NIV). Moses' reluctance angered God, but He listened and appointed Aaron to be Moses' spokesperson. Here we see two good friends who got "annoyed" with each other, yet continued to love each other and fellowship together.

The first time Moses asked Pharaoh to let the Israelites go, Pharaoh responded by increasing the slaves' workload. Moses then complained to God: *"O Lord, why have You brought harm to this people? Why did You ever send me?"* (Exodus 5:22) God's response to Moses was beautiful. He encouraged Moses first by reminding him of the promises that He had made to the Israelites, and then by repeating His promise to bring the people out of Egypt and into their Promised Land.

Have you ever thought you were doing God's will, only to have things turn out differently from what you expected? That is the time to go back to God and tell Him how you feel. Ask Him why things aren't working out the way you thought they would. Let Him encourage and comfort you. You may not know the whole picture. It may be that you are indeed doing His will, but that He has other purposes than just yours that He is working out.

When we care about someone, we want to know everything there is to know about that person. That's how Moses felt about God. His deep desire to know and understand God led him one day to ask the Lord, *"Now therefore, I pray You, if I have found favor in Your sight, let me know Your ways that I may know You, so that I may find favor in Your sight"* (Exodus 33:13). If you want a deep friendship with God, you need to get to know Him.

As Moses led the people through dangers and hardships, there were many times he lost his patience with their complaints and bickering. They complained about the food and the water, or the lack of them; they complained about their wilderness environment; they complained about Moses and his leadership. They even complained about the manna God sent to them daily. Despite the miraculous nature of this provision, the people grumbled because they were bored with having the same food every day.

Chapter 11 of Numbers records a wonderful conversation between God and Moses. Both of them were growing weary of these people who were never satisfied. Moses was upset, and he let God know exactly how he felt. Such is the freedom of true friendship:

> *So Moses said to the Lord, "Why have You been so hard on Your servant? And why have I not found favor in Your sight, that You have laid the burden of all this people on me? Was it I who conceived all this people? Was it I who brought them forth, that You should say to me, 'Carry them in your bosom as a nurse carries a nursing infant, to the*

> *land which You swore to their fathers'? Where am I to get meat to give to all this people? For they weep before me, saying, 'Give us meat that we may eat!' I alone am not able to carry all this people, because it is too burdensome for me. So if You are going to deal thus with me, please kill me at once, if I have found favor in Your sight, and do not let me see my wretchedness"* (Numbers 11:11–15).

Moses had had enough. The people's constant bickering and complaining, as well as their unending problems that needed to be resolved, had worn Moses down until he was ready to quit. God's response to Moses' tirade is a wonderful example of patience, love, compassion, and understanding:

> *The* Lord *therefore said to Moses, "Gather for Me seventy men from the elders of Israel, whom you know to be the elders of the people and their officers and bring them to the tent of meeting, and let them take their stand there with you. Then I will come down and speak with you there, and I will take of the Spirit who is upon you, and will put Him upon them; and they shall bear the burden of the people with you, so that you will not bear it all alone"* (Numbers 11:16–17).

Isn't it great to know that God understands your burdens? When was the last time you fell into the trap of thinking you had to manage everything alone? God gave you a task to do and you assumed you had to come up with the energy, patience, and wisdom to follow through in your own strength. How much better it would be to just be honest with God and tell Him how tired or frustrated you are. God hears you when you speak to Him as a trusted friend and tell Him exactly how you feel. He does not expect you to carry the burdens of this life alone. Go to Him in faith, get into fellowship with Him, and be honest about your feelings. As He did with Moses, God will lighten your burdens.

Advising God

One surprising aspect of Moses' friendship with God is that on occasion he was able to comfort God! When it was time for the Israelites to go into the land of Canaan, the people balked out of fear of the armies they would be facing. Rebelling against Moses (and God) they proposed choosing a new leader to take them back to Egypt. This latest mutiny was the last straw. Greatly angered, God seemed ready to wipe them out and start over:

> *The* L*ORD* *said to Moses, "How long will this people spurn Me? And how long will they not believe in Me, despite all the signs which I have performed in their midst? I will smite them with pestilence and dispossess them, and I will make you into a nation greater and mightier than they"* (Numbers 14:11–12).

Immediately, Moses began interceding for his people, even offering what sounded like "advice" for God. He reminded God that His reputation was at stake:

> *But Moses said to the* L*ORD*, *"Then the Egyptians will hear of it, for by Your strength You brought up this people from their midst, and they will tell it to the inhabitants of this land. They have heard that You, O* L*ORD*, *are in the midst of this people, for You, O* L*ORD*, *are seen eye to eye, while Your cloud stands over them; and You go before them in a pillar of cloud by day and in a pillar of fire by night. Now if You slay this people as one man, then the nations who have heard of Your fame will say, 'Because the* L*ORD* *could not bring this people into the land which He promised them by oath, therefore He slaughtered them in the wilderness' "* (Numbers 14:13–16).

Have you ever given advice to God? Does the very idea sound presumptuous? It is a strange thought that God might actually listen to or accept our "advice." Because God is omniscient (all-knowing), He certainly does not need us to tell Him what to do, but He does desire our friendship, and friends are always honest with each other.

God also wants us to listen to Him and to understand His ways. Because Moses had walked so intimately with God for so long, he knew God's plans and methods. As a result, Moses' "advice" to God was absolutely in line with God's own design. Moses was actually quoting God's own words back to Him:

> *But now, I pray, let the power of the* L*ORD* *be great, just as You have declared, "The* L*ORD* *is slow to anger and abundant in lovingkindness, forgiving iniquity and transgression; but He will by no means clear the guilty, visiting the iniquity of the fathers on the children to the third*

> *and the fourth generations." Pardon, I pray, the iniquity of this people according to the greatness of Your lovingkindness, just as You also have forgiven this people, from Egypt even until now* (Numbers 14:17–19).

With those words, Moses was simply reminding God of the promises that He had made and of the words that He had spoken. God must have been delighted to see that Moses knew Him so well! As a result of Moses' boldness, God forgave the people!

Friends First

How did such a remarkable relationship come to be? What could motivate a man as humble as Moses to offer "advice" to God, and have his advice followed?

Moses entered into a relationship with God. As it is with all of us, God *initiated* the relationship with Moses. None of us can come to know the Lord until and unless He reveals Himself to us. God revealed Himself personally to Moses at the burning bush. There He called Moses to his mission as the deliverer of the Israelites.

> "God desires our friendship."

More important than his mission, however, was Moses' personal relationship to the God who called him. That day at the burning bush, Moses embarked on a spiritual journey that lasted the rest of his life. He entered into fellowship with God, began talking with God, learned to obey God's commands, and walked faithfully with God. Over time, Moses' relationship with the Lord became so intimate and personal that the Bible would depict him as one of God's friends.

Next, Moses dedicated himself to God's plan. Remember, God offered to destroy the Israelites and raise up another nation of Moses' descendants. What glory that would have given to Moses! Moses, however, knew that this was not in God's perfect plan. His "advice" to God focused on bringing glory to God, not to himself.

Moses based his advice on God's own words and promises. He did not make a plan of his own. Instead, he listened to God and stored God's Word in his heart with firm faith that every one of God's promises would be kept.

I ask you again, have you ever given God advice? Have you ever said something like this: "Now, Lord, You really need to do this miracle for me"? If you have any thought of trying to give "advice" to the Lord, make sure you follow Moses' example first. Spend time with God becoming His friend. Store His Word in your heart, and dedicate yourself to His glory, not your own. All these things will strengthen your faith and relationship with God so that when you come to Him with your prayers, they will be in line with His desires. When these things are in place, prayers get answered!

Friendship with God is its own end and its own reward. Honestly, what more could you or any of us desire than to know the Lord of the universe in an intimate and thoroughly personal way?

A Simple Goal

The New Testament also has its "heroes" who walked with God. Of these, the apostle Paul is certainly one of the greatest. We tend to think of Paul primarily as the man who carried the Gospel to the Gentile world, who established and encouraged many of the early churches, and who wrote divinely inspired letters that have instructed and guided believers for nearly two thousand years.

If you had asked Paul what his life's work was, he would not have mentioned preaching or starting churches or writing epistles. These activities were the outgrowth—the fruit—of his life's work. Paul's life's work—the greatest longing of his heart—was simply to fellowship with Christ. He stated this emphatically in his letter to the Philippians:

> *I count all things to be loss in view of the surpassing value of knowing Christ Jesus my Lord, for whom I have suffered the loss of all things, and count them but rubbish so that I may gain Christ, and may be found in Him, not having a righteousness of my own derived from the Law, but that which is through faith in Christ, the righteousness which comes from God on the basis of faith, that I may know Him and the power of His resurrection and the fellowship of His sufferings, being conformed to His death; in order that I may attain to the resurrection from the dead. Not that I have already obtained it or have already become perfect, but I press on so that I may lay hold of that for which also I was laid hold of by Christ Jesus. Brethren, I do*

> *not regard myself as having laid hold of it yet; but one thing I do: forgetting what lies behind and reaching forward to what lies ahead, I press on toward the goal for the prize of the upward call of God in Christ Jesus* (Philippians 3:8–14).

Paul dedicated himself to knowing God. That was his first priority. The result was a deep and unshakable faith that was so glorious that Paul was impelled to share it with others. Out of his fellowship with Christ came a faith and a ministry that changed the world. This was not an instant or overnight achievement. Throughout his life, even to its very end, Paul was pressing on "*toward the goal*" of growing deeper in his relationship with Christ.

Fellowship with God is a lifelong project. Everything else must be subordinate to it. It is too easy to slip into the "works" mode and forget the relationship. If your fellowship time with God leads you to volunteer at your church or to testify to unbelievers, then you have your priorities straight. Be vigilant, however, that your good works don't take up so much time and energy that you neglect your personal relationship with God.

I really enjoy teaching Bible school students who are serious and committed—hungry and purposeful to know God's Word and His Son Jesus in a personal way. Through the years, however, I have watched people backslide while in Bible school, and have wondered, "How can that happen when they receive in-depth Bible teaching daily?"

After questioning some of them, and through prayer, I have discovered that, as strange as it seems, Bible students often neglect their own personal daily relationship with the Lord in the mistaken assumption that their Bible classes take the place of their personal time with God.

What a dangerous mistake! Each one of us, no matter who we are or what our calling is, must maintain a close, daily personal relationship with our loving Lord. Our spiritual health and welfare depend on it! Whenever we allow ourselves to become overburdened with things of the world—work, family, problems, relationships, financial difficulties, etc.—we tend to "shelve" the reading of the Word and our personal walks with God. It may make worldly sense to put God "on hold," but it never makes sense spiritually.

How much does God want your friendship? Again and again in the Bible, God made a way for fallen man to return to Him. He provided a sacrifice for Adam and Eve, made a covenant with Abraham, gave the law to Israel, and finally, sent His own Son: *"For God so loved the world, that He gave His only begotten Son, that whoever believes in Him shall not perish, but have eternal life"* (John 3:16).

Why did God send Jesus? *"God is faithful, through whom you were called into fellowship with His Son, Jesus Christ our Lord"* (1 Corinthians 1:9). God desires your fellowship so much that He even gave His only Son to restore your relationship with Him!

Who Wants to Be My Friend?

No matter who we are, sometimes we get down on ourselves and feel like failures. At such times it is hard to imagine anyone wanting to be our friend. Harder still is believing that a perfect God, the King of kings and Lord of lords, wants to be our friend. Nevertheless, the Bible tells us that God is the one who is reaching out to us, choosing to dwell in us and fellowship with us.

God said to the Israelites, *"I will dwell among the sons of Israel and will be their God"* (Exodus 29:45). After the Babylonian captivity, during the restoration of the temple, God gave us another assurance of His desire to dwell among us: *" 'Sing for joy and be glad, O daughter of Zion; for behold I am coming and I will dwell in your midst,' declares the LORD"* (Zechariah 2:10).

Jesus relates to us on an even more intimate level—as friends. Again, the choice is His, not ours:

> *You are My friends, if you do what I command you. No longer do I call you slaves, for the slave does not know what his master is doing; but I have called you friends, for all things that I have heard from My Father I have made known to you. You did not choose Me but I chose you, and appointed you that you would go and bear fruit, and that your fruit would remain, so that whatever you ask of the Father in My name He may give to you* (John 15:14–16).

Do you remember how it felt when you wished and hoped that the "coolest" and most popular kids in school would choose you as a friend? Look again at this Scripture; the coolest person of all—Jesus Christ—has chosen you as His friend!

What's the Catch?

Have you ever had a friend who took advantage of you? Perhaps she borrowed money from you and never repaid it. Maybe he moved in with you, ate your food, messed up your house, and never lifted a hand to help with either the work or the expenses. Even worse, your friend may have gossiped about you behind your back and damaged your reputation. Aside from trying to deal with the anger and hurt, what did you do?

> "There are conditions to fellowshiping with God."

As a Christian, you can and should still love and pray for a friend like that, but you don't have to continue to spend time with someone who abuses you. Healthy people set sensible boundaries on their relationships.

In the same way, God, in His infinite wisdom, established standards of friendship with Him. He wants your fellowship, but there are conditions.

God did not give us the Ten Commandments to make Himself feel powerful and important! He established those laws for our own good. His statutes grew out of His love and concern for us. Would a good friend ignore or reject such a gift?

One of the conditions of friendship with God is obedience to His laws:

> *If you walk in My statutes and keep My commandments so as to carry them out…I will also walk among you and be your God, and you shall be My people* (Leviticus 26:3, 12).

The second condition of fellowship is to walk in the light. Jesus is the Light of the world. Walking in the light means walking where He walks, walking where His Word leads us. If we continue to walk in darkness, we do not have fellowship with God or with one another:

> *This is the message we have heard from Him and announce to you, that God is Light, and in Him there is no darkness at all. If we say that we have fellowship with Him and yet walk in the darkness, we lie and do not practice the truth; but if we walk in the Light as He Himself is in the Light, we have fellowship with one another, and the blood of Jesus His Son cleanses us from all sin* (1 John 1:5–7).

Our walk with God will produce powerful results. As our fellowship deepens, so will our faith. As our faith grows, so will our desire for fellowship. Being friends with God is such a wonderful experience that we could be satisfied with that alone, but our God is a God of abundance. Fellowship with God brings many other blessings.

The Heavens Will Open

As you grow closer to God, you will be filled with the desire to obey Him. God wants love and fellowship, not blind obedience. Your willing obedience is a sign of your love and fellowship with Him:

> *Now, Israel, what does the LORD your God require from you, but to fear the LORD your God, to walk in all His ways and love Him, and to serve the LORD your God with all your heart and with all your soul, and to keep the LORD's commandments and His statutes which I am commanding you today for your good?* (Deuteronomy 10:12-13)

When you practice obedience to the Lord, physical and material prosperity follow. Deuteronomy 28 lists some of the blessings promised to the obedient, and they are fabulous!

> *Now it shall be, if you diligently obey the LORD your God, being careful to do all His commandments which I command you today, the LORD your God will set you high above all the nations of the earth. All these blessings will come upon you and overtake you if you obey the LORD your God: Blessed shall you be in the city, and blessed shall you be in the country. Blessed shall be the offspring of your body and the produce of your ground and the offspring of your beasts, the increase of your herd and the young of your flock. Blessed shall be your basket and your kneading bowl. Blessed shall you be when you come in, and blessed shall you be when you go out* (Deuteronomy 28:1–6).

You Will Bear Fruit

As you continue to fellowship with God and "actualize" His abiding in your life, you will bear fruit. In other words, as the presence of Christ in your life becomes more and more real to you, it affects everything you do: your efforts are fruitful; you accomplish what you set out to do; and you have the energy to fulfill what God wants of you. Learn to let Jesus live His life through you!

> *Abide in Me, and I in you. As the branch cannot bear fruit of itself unless it abides in the vine, so neither can you unless you abide in Me. I am the vine, you are the branches; he who abides in Me and I in him, he bears much fruit, for apart from Me you can do nothing* (John 15:4–5).

These verses remind me of Freda Lindsay, who was president of Christ for the Nations. Freda found the Lord at a very young age. She was never a "yo-yo" Christian—up one day and down the next. From the time she met the Lord, she literally grafted herself onto the living vine! She stuck to His Word. She was in constant fellowship with Him. In fact, she once told me that she has read through her Bible 52 times!

When Freda's husband Gordon passed away, she took on the awesome responsibility of directing the school's ministry, even though she felt incapable of the task. God alone gave her the wisdom to successfully guide this international organization.

As Freda shared this information with me, I thought, *So many times, we bear the fruit of who we are.* Christ for the Nations is a school where both youthful and older men and women come forth in the same power of God's Word and Spirit. Like Freda, these people learn to fellowship with the Lord, follow Him, and love Him with all their hearts.

Prayers Will Be Answered

Your power in prayer is directly related to your fellowship with God. It is not a "you be good and I will reward you" syndrome, but a life principle throughout the Word. Your walk, communion, and knowledge of God produce the power for answered prayer:

> *If you abide in Me, and My words abide in you, ask whatever you wish, and it will be done for you* (John 15:7).

As you come to know God better, you will begin to understand His ways—the methods He would choose to solve a problem. The more you know Him, the more God-like your prayers become. When your prayers are in line with His will, there is no doubt that they will be answered.

Believers Will Be United

As your fellowship with God brings you into line with His thinking, it also brings you into unity with others in the body of Christ. As believers, we all have the mind of Christ, but it is constant fellowship with Him that teaches us how to express His mind in our daily lives. As each member of the body learns more on how to express God's thoughts, clashes between us are diminished. This unity of believers is Christ's desire for His body, for this is how His bride, the church, prepares for His coming. Just before Judas' betrayal, Jesus prayed:

> *I pray also for those who will believe in Me through their message, that all of them may be one, Father, just as You are in Me and I am in You. May they also be in Us so that the world may believe that You have sent Me. I have given them the glory that You gave Me, that they may be one as We are one: I in them and You in Me. May they be brought to complete unity to let the world know that You sent Me and have loved them even as You have loved Me* (John 17:20–23 NIV).

Unity among believers is a sign to the world that Christ is the Son of God. When believers quarrel, become divided, and take sides against each other, it is a sure sign that we are not walking in fellowship with God. When we devote our time and energy to our friendship with Him, we become unified with other believers who are also walking with Him. *"The one who says he abides in Him ought himself to walk in the same manner as He walked"* (1 John 2:6). When we are all walking in the same direction—His direction—the world sees the wonder of God's love!

When Fellowship Is Broken

Fellowship is a two-way conversation. God already knows all there is to know about you, but He wants your voluntary communication. If you have sinned (as we all do every day, in some way) you must confess it to Him. He will wash away the guilt and instantly forget your sin—but first you must bring it to Him:

> *If we confess our sins, He is faithful and righteous to forgive us our sins and to cleanse us from all unrighteousness* (1 John 1:9).

Unconfessed sins in your life create a wall between you and God. They hinder your fellowship so that He cannot respond to your prayers. You may pray with what you call faith, but your prayer gets you nowhere. Sin has stopped communication between you and your God:

> *Behold, the* L*ORD's hand is not so short that it cannot save; nor is His ear so dull that it cannot hear. But your iniquities have made a separation between you and your God, and your sins have hidden His face from you so that He does not hear* (Isaiah 59:1–2).

After David sinned with Bathsheba, he kept the sin in his heart for months without repentance. His words in Psalm 32 express how he felt during this time:

> *When I kept silent about my sin, my body wasted away through my groaning all day long. For day and night Your hand was heavy upon me; my vitality was drained away as with the fever heat of summer* (Psalm 32:3–4).

David's fellowship with God had been broken. His prayers were not answered, and he felt like a sick man. It was only after he confessed his sin and received forgiveness that his fellowship with God was restored.

> "Unconfessed sin stops faith from working in your life."

If you are troubled by unanswered prayer, make sure there is no cause for broken fellowship with your Lord. The source of your faith is God and His Word. If your fellowship with the source is broken, the supply of faith is also affected. As a believer, that source is within you in the Holy Spirit, but He cannot work in or through you when sin is in the way. Unconfessed sin stops faith from working in your life.

When you sin, the devil uses it as a wedge to try to control your life. He seeks to get you to spend your time going over every wrong thing you ever did. He loves it when you send yourself into a pit of despair and self-pity.

Another technique that Satan uses is to get you so busy with your affairs that you barely notice when you have sinned. Don't listen to the voice of a liar. Listen instead to the voice of the Holy Spirit. When you know you have sinned, don't cover it up with an excuse or blame it on someone else. Call it what it is—sin.

For instance, if you have been lax in your prayer life, acknowledge your sin and ask forgiveness. Luke 21:36 (NKJV) tells us to *"pray always."* If He has shown you that you have not been praying as He said, you cannot say to God, "But, You know how busy I have been." You can say, "I have been disobedient; I have put other things ahead of my fellowship with You. Please forgive my sin."

Even if you have sinned, there is good news: Your fellowship can be restored instantly! God is always waiting with love and an open heart to welcome you back. Genuine confession of sin, however, also involves repentance.

Repentance means to turn around—turning *from* sin and turning *to* God. It is more than just a verbal recitation of offenses—it is a life-changing process. The way back to fellowship is to accept your responsibility for sin, confess it to Him, and then trust Him to forgive it completely.

Each day your fellowship with God should be growing more precious. Your time with Him should become the number one priority in your life. The more you walk in the light of His Word, the more treasures from it He will reveal to you. He also will reveal His plans for your life—a vision of the work He wants to do through you. It is the life of Christ that meets the needs of others through you. He is reaching out to you, asking you to walk in fellowship with Him. Accept His invitation. You have a Friend in high places! Be strong in your fellowship with the Lord. Guard it carefully and jealously. It will make you strong in your faith in Him! Your life will never be the same!

STEPS TO A SIMPLER FAITH

1. Tell God that you want and need His friendship. Commit to talk with Him at least ten minutes every day. As your fellowship grows, you will find yourself spending more and more time with Him.

2. In your journal or Scripture notebook, list five ways in which you are walking in the Light and the ways that you are still walking in darkness.

3. Read and meditate on Psalm 51. List what steps David took in his prayer to the Lord. Share these steps with a friend.

4. Commit to reading through the Bible in a year. As you read daily, write down new revelation. What does God say He will do? What does God say you are to do? Who does God say He

is? Who does God say you are? What is He like? What are His desires? What are His methods? What are His plans?

5. Look up forgiveness in a concordance and write down as many verses as you can that deal with this subject. Meditate on how you can put them into practice this week.

CHAPTER ELEVEN

Faith—The Gateway to Prosperity

One charming quality about children is their absolute faith in their parents' ability to give them anything! In their minds, money is no object and nothing is out of reach. Whatever they need or want, they believe without question that Mommy and Daddy can get it for them.

As they grow older and learn more of the realities of life, children realize that things are not as simple as they once believed. They discover that Mommy and Daddy don't have an endless supply of money and cannot buy them every new toy that comes along.

It is different in the spiritual realm. This childlike quality of absolute confidence in a parent's ability to provide is a critical part of effective faith. As Christians, we really do have a Father who can provide us with *anything* because He possesses unlimited resources. Like little children, we need to trust God for our prosperity in every area of life.

God wants us to prosper spiritually, physically, and financially. He does not want us to settle for "just enough." Instead, He wants to pour down so many blessings on us that our storehouse overflows!

John expressed our Lord's concern for our overall prosperity this way: *"Beloved, I pray that in all respects you may prosper and be in good health, just as your soul prospers"* (3 John 2). As this is part of the Word of God, it reflects His heart and desire for us. One way to look at this verse is to identify three areas of prosperity: **financial** (*"I pray that…you may prosper"*); **physical** (*"and be in good health"*); and **spiritual** (*"as your soul prospers"*).

The prosperity of God's children is one of the themes of the Bible. From the very beginning, God gave Adam prosperity. In the Garden of Eden, Adam could find everything he needed for abundant living. Later, God made a covenant with His chosen people, and prosperity was a big part of His promise to the Israelites:

> *The LORD will make you abound in prosperity, in the offspring of your body and in the offspring of your beast and in the produce of your ground, in the land which the LORD swore to your fathers to give you* (Deuteronomy 28:11).

God conferred upon the Israelites the power to acquire wealth so that they could demonstrate to the world the power and generosity of their God as well as His faithfulness in keeping promises:

> *But you shall remember the LORD your God, for it is He who is giving you power to make wealth, that He may confirm His covenant which He swore to your fathers, as it is this day* (Deuteronomy 8:18).

"God's biblical promises apply to all His children in every age."

God's biblical promises apply to all His children in every age. This means that just as He did for the Israelites, God also has given you the power to make wealth. He has already wrapped your gift! It is not a stingy little gift, but unlimited treasure. God wants you to rejoice over the blessings He sends you:

> *Let them shout for joy and rejoice, who favor my vindication; and let them say continually, "The LORD be magnified, who delights in the prosperity of His servant"* (Psalm 35:27).

Beware, however, for there will always be someone who wants to steal what you have. Satan is a thief who comes to *"steal and kill and destroy"* (John 10:10). He tries to steal your wealth by convincing you that you don't deserve it. He loves to discourage you in your efforts until you decide, "Well, I'm just supposed to be poor." How can you protect your prosperity from the thief? How can you appropriate the prosperity that God wants to shower upon you?

To live in biblical prosperity, you must walk in the truth. Right after his prayer for his readers' prosperity, John says:

> *For I was very glad when brethren came and testified to your truth, that is, how you are walking in truth. I have no greater joy than this, to hear of my children walking in the truth* (3 John 3–4).

Walking in truth will build your faith and cause you to prosper in every way.

It is important for you to believe that God wants you to prosper. People sometimes say, "Well, Jesus is my example, and He was poor, so I am supposed to be poor." There is a difference between Jesus as our *example* and Jesus as our *substitute*.

Jesus is our *example* as a servant. We are to serve others as He did. He is also our *example* in love and authority and dominion. We are to walk in His steps in all of these things. When Jesus went to the cross to pay for our sins, however, He was acting as our *substitute*. We are not to take on the sins or sicknesses of others; indeed, we cannot. As our substitute, only Jesus could take on our sins. In this, He was not setting an example for us to follow.

Jesus is also our substitute in poverty. He did not live as a poor man to set an example for us. He became poor so that we might be rich. Prosperity is our covenant right: *"For you know the grace of our Lord Jesus Christ, that though He was rich, yet for your sake He became poor, so that you through His poverty might become rich"* (2 Corinthians 8:9).

To receive your blessings you need to claim them. Several years ago, a pastor in Niagara Falls told me of a time when his area desperately needed rain. Many of the men in his congregation were farmers and their situation had been growing steadily worse. Without rain, all of the crops would be ruined. The pastor reminded his congregation that God did not desire poverty and hard times to fall upon them; He wanted them to prosper. After studying the promises in the Bible, the congregation began to pray and ask God to deliver the prosperity that He promised. Rain came and the crops were saved!

Deposits in the Bank of Heaven

What is the best way to save money? Should you hide cash in the back of a drawer somewhere? The drawback to that approach is that it will never grow. When you retrieve it several weeks or months later, there will still be only the amount you originally put there. In the meantime, inflation may have even decreased its value. There is also the possibility that someone could come along and steal your money, leaving you with nothing.

In order for your money to grow, you must invest it in instruments or vehicles that will bring the largest positive returns. That which you invest in God's kingdom will return the very highest rates of all and come back to you multiplied many times. Jesus had more to say on the subject of money and money management than on any other single topic because He knew the powerful hold money can have on our hearts. During the Sermon on the Mount He warned:

> *Do not store up for yourselves treasures on earth, where moth and rust destroy, and where thieves break in and steal. But store up for yourselves treasures in heaven, where neither moth nor rust destroys, and where thieves do not break in or steal; for where your treasure is, there your heart will be also* (Matthew 6:19–21).

As Christians and citizens of the kingdom of God, we each have an "account" in the "bank" of heaven into which we can deposit the kinds of incorruptible treasures that Jesus was talking about—deposits that will bring abundant and eternal returns.

Where money is concerned, there are essentially three ways to make a deposit into your heavenly account: tithes, offerings, and alms.

Tithing is a part of God's covenant of blessing. Although we need to recognize that God is the owner and source of all that we have, we also need to acknowledge that tithing specifically means giving back to God ten percent of everything He has given us. The Israelites presented their tithes to the high priest. Since Jesus is our great High Priest, we should present our tithes to Him and in His name. Bringing our tithes to the Lord is a way of blessing Him. Tithing is a spiritual law, and as such, carries a reward with it:

> *Honor the* Lord *from your wealth and from the first of all your produce; so your barns will be filled with plenty, and your vats will overflow with new wine* (Proverbs 3:9–10).

When we tithe, we invest our income with Jesus. God has promised to fill our every need, but He also goes much farther than that:

> *"Bring the whole tithe into the storehouse, so that there may be food in My house, and test Me now in this," says the* Lord *of hosts, "if I will not open for you the windows of heaven and pour out for you a blessing until it overflows"* (Malachi 3:10).

In this passage, the word *windows* means "flood gates." Your blessings won't just trickle down; they will inundate you; they will absolutely overwhelm you! Tithing is the first step to investing in your heavenly prosperity account.

God honors and provides for those who are faithful with the tithe. Sometimes He does it in totally unexpected ways. I know a pastor in Lisbon, Portugal, whose congregation numbers over 40,000. His Angolan ministry is even larger: over 50,000. Pastor George, who is also an electrical engineer and architect, built a large church building. One week before the first conference was to take place in the new building, the government declared, "This building does not pass inspection! We are tearing it down!" Bulldozers ripped away until the building was completely demolished.

When Pastor George heard the news, he did not backslide, scream, rebuke the devil, or curse God. Instead, He turned to the Lord. He said, "God, I put the very best into this church. I thought I was following Your will in building it. How did I miss it? Had I known it would just be torn down, I would have used inferior materials."

God replied, "I wanted you to use the best so I could bless you. Trust Me; this is your first fruit. The next nine-tenths will come easily." George relinquished the ruins as a sacrifice.

In the end, acting in response to international pressure regarding human rights violations, the Portuguese regime paid Pastor George *double* for the building and gave him even more land!

God promises that when we bring all our tithes into the storehouse, He will *"rebuke the devourer for your sakes, so that he will not destroy the fruit of your ground, nor shall the vine fail to bear fruit for you in the field"* (Malachi 3:11 NKJV). In the case of Pastor George and his church, God transformed an ugly political act into a great gift because they were faithful to give Him the best of the first fruits.

Spontaneous Deposits

Offerings are the gifts you give when the Holy Spirit nudges you to give above and beyond the tithe. These gifts may be to individuals or to ministries. The Holy Spirit will show you what to give and to whom.

Once, I needed a wristwatch and didn't tell anyone. I wanted God to provide it to me. Months went by and nothing happened. I simply kept praying and claiming the promise in Luke 6:38: *"Give, and it will be given to you. They will pour into your lap a good measure—pressed down, shaken together, and running over. For by your standard of measure it will be measured to you in return."* I reminded the Lord that I had been giving to needy people. On one occasion I had even given away our grocery money, and now I really needed a watch!

A few days later, just after Christmas, one of our deacons brought his wife over to me and said, "Marilyn, I want you to see a gift that I gave my wife for Christmas." It was a beautiful watch. I said, "Oh, that's a gorgeous watch!" Then he said "You know, the Lord has put it on my heart to give you a watch just like this." I replied, "And He has put it on my heart to receive it!"

God's law of prosperity says that what we give will be given back to us. He opens a way to return our generosity. Over the years, I have given many, many gifts, and I have received many, many gifts in return. It is beautiful to see what God will do for His people when we understand and follow His statutes.

Give to the Poor

God expects us to give tithes and He encourages us to give offerings. The third kind of spiritual investment of money is alms: giving to the poor. The Bible says, *"One who is gracious to a poor man lends to the LORD, and He will repay him for his good deed"* (Proverbs 19:17). Our gifts to the poor are really gifts to God. They go straight to His heart and result in His blessing us.

The book of Acts tells of Dorcas, who was known for her almsgiving and was raised from the dead by Peter (see Acts 9:36–42). Cornelius, a Roman centurion, also had a good reputation for giving alms and showing other acts of kindness and generosity. In response to his prayer, an angel of God told him, *"Your prayers and alms have ascended as a memorial before God"* (Acts 10:4). Because of his generous spirit and earnest seeking of spiritual truth, Cornelius and his entire household became some of the first Gentiles to hear and believe the Gospel and the first Gentiles to receive the baptism of the Holy Spirit. (See Acts 10:44–48.)

Giving alms brings marvelous results because sowing is based on the principle of multiplication. Just as one seed sown produces fruit and many new seeds for future harvests, sowing alms reaps manifold blessings from heaven.

An ungenerous, ungiving spirit is deadly to the soul. The Dead Sea is a prime example. With no outlet, the Dead Sea receives and receives and receives, but never gives anything back. The only way water escapes from the Dead Sea is through evaporation. This body of water truly lives up to its name. I have seen it, and believe me, you would not want to swim in it. The salt and chemical levels are so high that they can burn your skin. The Dead Sea has a terrible odor, and nothing can live in it or around it.

In order to have God's blessings flowing into us, we must have an outflow, or we become like the Dead Sea. Our hearts fill up with toxic waste and our lives really begin to stink!

The word *alms* means "mercy." Alms should be given in secret, or at least without any fanfare, but God will reward openly. There are many ways to sow alms to the poor besides giving money. You could volunteer your time to help someone in need. Offer to baby-sit for an overwhelmed single mother in your neighborhood. Make an extra casserole and leave it on the doorstep of an unemployed neighbor. Visit an elderly shut-in or run errands for someone recovering from an illness. Then watch your alms "flow back" to you!

Hilarious Giving

God is not interested in the dollar value of our gifts as much as He is the spirit and attitude with which we give it. Jesus made this crystal clear to His disciples one day:

> *And He looked up and saw the rich putting their gifts into the treasury. And He saw a poor widow putting in two small copper coins. And He said, "Truly I say to you, this poor widow put in more than all of them; for they all out of their surplus put into the offering; but she out of her poverty put in all that she had to live on"* (Luke 21:1–4).

This widow's two pennies meant little by the world's standard of measure, but it meant a great deal to God. By giving everything she had to live on, this woman was demonstrating that she loved God more than anything in the world and trusted Him to provide for her needs. That is simple, childlike faith—the kind of faith God looks for and honors.

Attitude is all-important when it comes to giving. Giving that honors God—and that God honors—comes from a willing and cheerful heart:

> *Now this I say, he who sows sparingly will also reap sparingly, and he who sows bountifully will also reap bountifully. Each one must do just as he has purposed in his heart, not grudgingly or under compulsion, for God loves a cheerful giver* (2 Corinthians 9:6–7).

The word *cheerful* in verse 7 literally means "hilarious." A cheerful giver is a "hilarious" giver. When you laugh "hilariously" you hold nothing back—you laugh with your whole being. Your giving is to be the same way. Give with every ounce of your heart, with no regrets, no second thoughts, and no feeling of obligation. When you give this way, your first reward will be a deep joy in your heart.

> "Attitude is all-important when it comes to giving."

In Matthew 20:1–16, Jesus tells a parable about a man who hired field hands to bring in his harvest. He hired some people in the morning and promised them a denarius for a day's work. He hired more workers at noon, and even more in the late afternoon. At the end of the day, he paid everyone the same amount. The ones who were hired early in the morning complained, "That's not fair. We worked a lot longer. Why did you pay the others the same amount as us?"

The man answered:

> *"Friend, I am doing you no wrong; did you not agree with me for a denarius? Take what is yours and go, but I wish to give to this last man the same as to you. Is it not lawful for me to do what I wish with what is my own? Or is your eye envious because I am generous?"* (Matthew 20:13–15)

This employer paid the later workers the same as the earlier ones because he wanted to; he had a generous spirit. Check your attitude. An ungenerous spirit will keep you in bondage. Small-mindedness will keep you poor.

When you sow generosity, you reap prosperity. This is the law of prosperity that God laid down. God knew when He sowed Jesus—one seed upon the earth—that Jesus would die and bring forth a harvest of many. Now Jesus wants to reward what you sow with a harvest of financial, physical, and spiritual prosperity.

Is It Godly to Be Poor?

Some Christians think it is a mark of godliness to be poor, or to just barely get along, but that is not God's desire for you. There is nothing *ungodly* about being poor, either. People in Jesus' day commonly believed that poverty was a curse from God because of sin, and that wealth was a sign of God's favor. Jesus made it clear in many of His teachings that this simply is not so. There were (and *are*) many ungodly rich people, as well as many godly people of very humble means. At the same time, there are many poor people who are just as materialistic and ungodly as many rich folk, while there are also many wealthy people who are humble and committed servants of Christ. The presence or absence of material wealth is not the issue. The issue is a person's *attitude* toward wealth.

The Bible also makes it clear, however, that God does not want His children to struggle from day to day to make ends meet. His desire is that we prosper in every way. Late in his life, David testified, *"I have been young, and now am old; yet I have not seen the righteous forsaken, nor his descendants begging bread"* (Psalm 37:25 NKJV). Paul reminded the Corinthians, *"For you know the grace of our Lord Jesus Christ, that though He was rich, yet for your sake He became poor, so that you through His poverty might become rich"* (2 Corinthians 8:9). This verse refers primarily to spiritual wealth, but it also takes in material prosperity.

Jesus Himself demonstrated this on more than one occasion. At the wedding feast in Cana, when Mary asked Jesus to make wine because the host had run out, did He make just enough to get by? No! He said, "Pour!" and when they poured, they had all the wine they needed and more, and it was better quality wine than the first wine had been. Once, when Peter and the other fishermen had fished all night without success, Jesus told them to let down their nets on the other side of the boat. When they did, they pulled in a haul of fish so great that the nets began to break. The Lord provided much more than they needed to "just get by." When Jesus fed five thousand people with three loaves of bread and two fish, He did not provide just a morsel for each person. No, everybody ate until they were full, and there were still twelve baskets of leftovers!

The wedding guests got wine because someone obeyed Jesus' command to pour. The fishermen got fish because they obeyed His command to cast out their nets. The people were fed because the disciples obeyed Jesus' command to set the bread before the five thousand. Our God is not the God of stinginess; He is the God of generosity and abundance. God does not want you to just "squeak by." He wants you to be enormously prosperous.

Put Christ First in Your Life

There is a condition to this prosperity, however. To receive Christ's abundance in this life, you must be in obedience to Him, and that means placing Him *first* in your life. Take care of His business and He will take care of yours. Trust Him and follow Him in every way, and He will provide for your needs. Jesus said:

> *Do not worry then, saying, "What will we eat?" or "What will we drink?" or "What will we wear for clothing?" For the Gentiles eagerly seek all these things; for your heavenly Father knows that you need all these things. But seek first His kingdom and His righteousness, and all these things will be added to you* (Matthew 6:31–33).

Start praising God right now for His provision. Delight in Him and seek Him. As you read your Bible, ask Him for the wisdom to see His way of doing things. Get in line with His heart, walk with Him in everything you do, and He will reward you:

> *For the LORD God is a sun and shield; the LORD gives grace and glory; no good thing does He withhold from those who walk uprightly* (Psalm 84:11).

In order to lay claim to the riches that God has stored up for you, you must surrender your worldly motivations for wanting wealth.

Pursuing wealth for its own sake or for selfish gratification is a worldly motivation. Even serving the Lord can be a worldly motivation if you serve Him *only* out of the desire for Him to prosper you. Put God *first*; trust, follow, and obey Him.

Your first priority is to keep your eyes on God, being alert and ready to bind the devil and his forces in the name of Jesus. Satan is a thief, and he will try to steal your prosperity with seeds of doubt and despair. Bind the devil and say, "You are not going to take away my prosperity!" Loose the forces of heaven to conquer Satan and bring in that prosperity.

Why Money?

Why does God want us to have wealth? God prospers us because He takes pleasure in doing so, but also so that we can be a financial blessing to others. The Lord uses our hands to do His work on earth. Therefore, if He wants to bless a person, He will most likely use another person to do so. We can become conduits for the riches of God. With His wealth we can establish His covenant. Money is not for the purpose of feeding our selfish lusts and desires, but for fulfilling God's purpose.

It is not *getting* that makes prosperity worth having; it is *giving* that makes prosperity worth getting. Did God prosper Joseph in Egypt so he could drive the Mercedes of his day—a golden chariot? God took Joseph from the prison to the palace to preserve the lives of his family the bloodline through which man's salvation—the Messiah, Jesus Christ—would come. Prosperity fulfills God's *first* priority—to win souls.

First, we receive, and then we give—to the work of God and to others. Then we receive back—probably through other people—and have enough to give again. Jesus said, *"Freely you have received, freely give"* (Matthew 10:8 NKJV).

Some people claim, misquoting the apostle Paul, that "money is the root of all evil." This is not true. In point of fact, Paul said, *"For the **love** of money is the root of all evil"* (1 Timothy 6:10 KJV). Money itself is neutral, neither good nor bad. Your attitude toward money is what will make the difference in your life. Either you own your money or it will own you. Check your motive. Do you desire wealth for your own worldly satisfaction, or do you want it for the advancement of God's purposes?

Jesus issued many warnings to the wealthy and of the dangers of wealth. The problem is not wealth itself, but the attitude so many wealthy people have toward their riches. For example, it is wrong and spiritually deadly to pursue wealth as the driving force of one's life, or to use it for selfish gain or to oppress others, particularly the poor and weak. On the other hand, wealth put to godly purposes—supporting missionaries, feeding the hungry, underwriting a Bible school or college—can bring great blessings to countless people around the world.

"Your attitude toward money is what will make the difference in your life."

The rich young ruler came to Jesus seeking the way to obtain eternal life. He thought he really wanted it—until he found out the price. Jesus told him to sell his possessions and give to the poor and come follow Him. The young man went away sorrowful because he could not do it. He was a slave to his riches. Parting with his wealth was necessary for *this* man to find eternal life because his wealth was standing in his way.

When Jesus told the rich young ruler to sell his possessions, He was addressing that man's specific problem; He was not establishing a universal principle for all believers to follow. Unless Jesus specifically and personally instructs us otherwise, it is not necessary to take a vow of poverty in order to follow Him. It *is* necessary to acknowledge Him as the source, owner, and Lord of all we have. Remember, He is the one who gives us the ability to make wealth.

True prosperity comes not from our efforts, but from God's generosity, and God-given prosperity is to be used to advance His kingdom. It is important to learn to see money through God's eyes. In God's economy, materialism and *love* of money corrupt the spirit and lead to death. Real prosperity comes out of the prosperity of the soul. Here are some important principles for looking at money the way God does:

- Renew your mind with a godly "money" outlook.
- Trust God, not money.
- Prevent money from manipulating you. Use money to please God, not man.
- Avoid (lust) consuming all your seed (money), or you will have nothing to plant.
- Make regular deposits in God's kingdom.

- Be frugal.
- Save a portion of all money you receive.
- Put a stop to credit—spending tomorrow's money today.
- Live below your means.
- Spend time planning, budgeting, and controlling your finances.
- Retire debt, so you are free to give.
- Get to give—then give away all you can.
- Invest in winning souls for Christ.
- Money is your servant. You are not money's servant.

Renewing Your Mind

God's prosperity is not only material. More importantly, He wants to prosper your soul. Jerry Savelle says in one of his books, "a prosperous soul is one in which the mind is renewed, the will conformed, the emotions controlled, and the thinking faculties selective of that which it thinks."[9] A prosperous soul encompasses your entire being—the "real you" inside your body. Without a prospering soul, material wealth will be fleeting.

The best way to renew your mind is to replace your thoughts with God's thoughts. His thoughts are much higher than yours, and they are much more effective:

> *"For My thoughts are not your thoughts, nor are your ways My ways," declares the* Lord. *"For as the heavens are higher than the earth, so are My ways higher than your ways and My thoughts than your thoughts"* (Isaiah 55:8–9).

When God made you a new creature, He also gave you Christ's mind:

> *For who has known or understood the mind (the counsels and purposes) of the Lord so as to guide and instruct Him and give Him knowledge? But we have the mind of Christ (the Messiah) and do hold the thoughts (feelings and purposes) of His heart* (1 Corinthians 2:16 AMP).

The way to experience the mind of Christ is to flood your mind with His Word! We are commanded to *"renew"* our mind. When we do, our souls will prosper!

Like all of us, you are constantly making choices. Every day you face hundreds of decisions. You can decide to do things your way, the world's way, or God's way. Everything you do is a choice. You can even choose not to choose! Paul said to the Romans:

> *Do not be conformed to this world, but be transformed by the renewing of your mind, so that you may prove what the will of God is, that which is good and acceptable and perfect* (Romans 12:2).

Get into the habit of asking with each choice you make, "Is this choice conformed to God's will?" If this goal seems overwhelming, remember that God has already given you the mind of Christ, and He will enable you to do His will: *"For it is God who is at work in you, both to will and to work for His good pleasure"* (Philippians 2:13). He gives you the desire to conform to His will. Yield to Him, and prosper your soul!

How could we describe the prosperous soul? Borrowing the words of the apostle Paul, we could say that a prosperous soul is a soul filled with the "fruit of the Spirit":

> *But the fruit of the Spirit is love, joy, peace, patience, kindness, goodness, faithfulness, gentleness, self-control; against such things there is no law* (Galatians 5:22–23).

As a believer, you already have the potential—the seed—for all this fruit in your soul right now. To bear this fruit productively in your life is a matter of switching from your way of thinking to Christ's way of thinking—from selfish control of your own life and mind to yielding to His control.

When your soul prospers, you walk in the wisdom of the Lord, thinking His kind of thoughts and living by His kind of faith. Conform your will to His by making the "quality decision" to choose God's ways. Control your emotions by remembering that Jesus is the source of everything you need in your life. His Spirit has positive emotional fruit for every negative feeling that comes your way.

Physical Prosperity

Walk in the Word of God in every area of your life! Some people understand that they are supposed to prosper spiritually, yet have not learned that God also wants them to prosper physically. Such an attitude is not in alignment with God's Word. How could a God who is the source of *all* prosperity prosper us in our finances and in our souls, but not in our bodies?

Our physical health was part of the reason Jesus came to earth: *"He Himself took our infirmities and carried away our diseases"* (Matthew 8:17). When Jesus went about preaching, He looked at the bodies of people as well as their souls. He was concerned with the prosperity of the whole person. Whenever He preached the Gospel, He also healed the sick and delivered the mentally tormented.

God reveals in His Word that He wants us to be healthy. He never said that we should bear up under sickness with a grim and determined patience. Jesus healed sickness whenever faith was present. The Word of God even instructs us to ask for healing:

> *Is anyone among you sick? Then he must call for the elders of the church and they are to pray over him, anointing him with oil in the name of the Lord; and the prayer offered in faith will restore the one who is sick, and the Lord will raise him up, and if he has committed sins, they will be forgiven him* (James 5:14–15).

God's desire is for us to prosper in health until the day we go home to be with Him: *"As your days, so shall your strength be"* (Deuteronomy 33:25 NKJV).

In way of a summary, here are seven principles or keys to attaining the prosperity in your life that God desires for you:

1. **Be obedient**: *"Therefore keep the words of this covenant and do them, that you may deal wisely and prosper in all that you do"* (Deuteronomy 29:9 AMP).
2. **Put God first**: *"But seek (aim at and strive after) first of all His kingdom and His righteousness (His way of doing and being right), and then all these things taken together will be given you besides"* (Matthew 6:33 AMP).

3. **Be diligent in all things**: *"He becomes poor who works with a slack and idle hand, but the hand of the diligent makes rich"* (Proverbs 10:4 AMP).
4. **Use God's wisdom**: *"Riches and honor are with me, enduring wealth and righteousness (uprightness in every area and relation, and right standing with God)"* (Proverbs 8:18 AMP).
5. **Have a right attitude toward God**: *"O taste and see that the LORD is good; how blessed is the man who takes refuge in Him! O fear the LORD, you His saints; for to those who fear Him there is no want. The young lions do lack and suffer hunger; but they who seek the LORD shall not be in want of any good thing"* (Psalm 34:8–10).
6. **Meditate on the Word**: *"But his delight is in the law of the LORD, and in His law he meditates day and night. He will be like a tree firmly planted by streams of water, which yields its fruit in its season and its leaf does not wither; and in whatever he does, he prospers"* (Psalm 1:2–3).
7. **Tithe, give, and care for God's house**: *" 'Bring the whole tithe into the storehouse, so that there may be food in My house, and test Me now in this,' says the LORD of hosts, 'if I will not open for you the windows of heaven and pour out for you a blessing until it overflows' "* (Malachi 3:10).

The key to receiving God's prosperity is perseverance. You cannot afford to get discouraged.

The next time you feel like you are losing everything, remember that your heavenly Father is the owner of unlimited resources. He has promised to supply all your needs according to His riches in glory. The key is faithfulness, perseverance, and obedience. Don't worry about your daily needs. Like a little child, trust your Father to provide. He really can and He really will—a bountiful supply!

STEPS TO A SIMPLER FAITH

1. Meditate on the seven keys to prosperity and the accompanying verses. In your journal write out what you can do to receive God's blessings.

2. Read about the fruit of the Spirit in Galatians 5:22–23. Think of ways you can share God's emotions (rather than your own) with an unsaved loved one or friend.
3. Compare and contrast how one's attitude toward riches affects prosperity, using Matthew 6:19–24, 25:40–45; Luke 6:38; 12:15; and 2 Corinthians 9:6–10.
4. Pray for financial wisdom. Ask God where you can cheerfully invest in His kingdom and whom you should bless financially.
5. Where do you need healing? Memorize one of the following verses to remind you that God heals all aspects of your life: Psalm 103:2–3; Isaiah 61:1; Jeremiah 3:22, 30:17; Hosea 6:1; Malachi 4:2.

CHAPTER TWELVE

Faith That Changes Hearts and Minds

One of the biggest challenges many of us face when it comes to our faith is maintaining confidence that the purposes of God will prevail in a world that seems more godless, lost, and defiant than ever. Evil and spiritual darkness grow more oppressive; hunger, poverty, and disease are still on the rise in many parts of the world; and hostility toward the Gospel of Christ and violence against His followers are becoming more and more commonplace worldwide.

This should not surprise us. After all, the New Testament clearly states that times will grow darker before the return of Christ. Paul warned that people would turn away from the truth in favor of teachings that would accommodate and encourage them in their own sinful and selfish desires (see 2 Timothy 4:3–4). He described those who deny the truth as

> *Being filled with all unrighteousness, wickedness, greed, evil; full of envy, murder, strife, deceit, malice; they are gossips, slanderers, haters of God, insolent, arrogant, boastful, inventors of evil, disobedient to parents, without understanding, untrustworthy, unloving, unmerciful* (Romans 1:29–31).

Even though Paul wrote these words nearly two thousand years ago, he could be describing our world of the twenty-first century!

What hope do we have in such times? Can our faith actually survive against such an epidemic of evil? More than that, can we thrive and prevail in spite of the persistent godlessness around us? The answer is yes!

Jesus told His disciples, *"These things I have spoken to you, so that in Me you may have peace. In the world you have tribulation, but take courage; I have overcome the world"* (John 16:33). He was trying to encourage them while at the same time prepare them for what lay ahead. Even though the disciples would know hardship, trouble, and persecution as Jesus' followers, they also would know His peace, His presence, and His power to overcome. No matter what they endured at the hands of the world, in the end, they—and their message—would prevail.

The same is true for us. Regardless of how things appear from time to time, if we walk steadfastly by faith and keep our hearts and minds focused on Jesus, we will be victorious. That is the Lord's promise to us.

There is another reason for the prevalence and apparent increase of evil and godlessness in our day. We live in a time when the greatest spiritual awakenings in the history of man are occurring. The Spirit of God is moving mightily in the earth and lost people are coming to Christ in greater numbers than ever before. This has galvanized Satan and his forces to a desperate fury of activity. The brighter the light shines, the harder the darkness works to suppress it.

God's purposes will never be defeated. All that He desires will come to pass. What does God desire? Jesus stated it perfectly to Nicodemus:

> *For God so loved the world, that He gave His only begotten Son, that whoever believes in Him shall not perish, but have eternal life. For God did not send the Son into the world to judge the world, but that the world might be saved through Him* (John 3:16–17).

In his first letter to Timothy, Paul described God's desire and also indicated what our part as believers is to be in relation to that desire:

> *I urge, then, first of all, that requests, prayers, intercession and thanksgiving be made for everyone—for kings and all those in authority, that we may live peaceful and quiet lives in all godliness and holiness. This is good, and pleases God our Savior, who wants all men to be saved and to come to a knowledge of the truth* (1 Timothy 2:1–4 NIV).

God's desire is for *"all men to be saved and to come to a knowledge of the truth." Our* responsibility—*"first of all"*—is to pray. When we pray, we put our faith to work, and when we put our faith to work, God accomplishes His purposes in the world.

How Does God Work?

How does this work in practical reality? Does praying for other people or situations really make a difference? Can you effectively pray in faith for someone whose will is opposed to the answer? Make no mistake, many times your prayers will be in direct conflict to another person's will in a given situation. For example, you may pray for the restoration of a marriage when one or the other partner has already given up on it and entered into another relationship. You may pray for the return of a rebellious child who is making decisions contrary to God's Word. This child may be living outside of God's will and has told you many times that he or she does not want to follow God. Can you pray with faith for God to change that person's will and be confident it will happen?

Often, when we pray for something that is against someone else's will, we tend to say, "Well, I prayed in faith; now it is up to that individual and God. My part is over." If our prayer is not answered, we can easily blame it on the other person's unwillingness to yield to God. After all, he or she had free will in the situation and chose not to follow the Lord. On the surface this sounds reasonable, but is this really the way God works?

When Christ was raised from the dead, God gave Him a name that is above every name, seated Him at His right hand, and put all things under His feet. All authority was given to Him. Paul says in Ephesians that God

> *...raised* [Christ] *from the dead and seated Him at His right hand in the heavenly places, far above all rule and authority and power and dominion, and every name that is named, not only in this age but also in the one to come. And He put all things in subjection under His feet, and gave Him as head over all things to the church, which is His body, the fullness of Him who fills all in all* (Ephesians 1:20–23).

Jesus then transferred His authority to His church. He gave us His name as "power of attorney" to do His will on earth. We are to act as

His representatives, in His name. Just before Jesus left this earth and ascended to His Father, He gave us our marching orders:

> *All authority has been given to Me in heaven and on earth. Go therefore and make disciples of all the nations, baptizing them in the name of the Father and the Son and the Holy Spirit, teaching them to observe all that I commanded you; and lo, I am with you always, even to the end of the age* (Matthew 28:18–20).

Jesus came with authority and sends us out in His authority. He said to His Father, *"As You sent Me into the world, I also have sent them into the world"* (John 17:18). After His resurrection, He repeated this commission to His disciples: *"Peace be with you; as the Father has sent Me, I also send you"* (John 20:21). Jesus is seated at the right hand of His Father in heaven, but He is working down here on earth through His body, the church. He has made His will clear in His Word and has given the church the power and authority to do His will. Now He waits for the church to do her part.

> "Jesus is waiting for us to do our part."

We are the body of Christ, of which He is the head. A body cannot survive, let alone function, without its head. Neither can we as the body of Christ survive or function without Him. Sometimes, however, we forget or fail to understand that our head has *chosen* to work through His body. John 15:4 says that the branches cannot bear fruit unless they are attached to the vine. At the same time, the vine cannot bear fruit without the branches. Can you believe it? The Lord has chosen *us*—you, me, and every other member of His body—to accomplish His work on earth! It is almost incomprehensible!

We Have the Power

Jesus has given us His authority, and this includes authority over Satan. When Jesus defeated Satan on the cross, He stripped him of his power and authority over us. Then He turned the tables on the devil, giving *us* authority over *him*. Because we are Christ's representatives on earth, we can bind or loose here that which is bound or loosed in heaven. Jesus said:

> *I will give you the keys of the kingdom of heaven; and whatever you bind on earth shall have been bound in heaven, and whatever you loose on earth shall have been loosed in heaven* (Matthew 16:19).

This means that we have received from Jesus the authority on earth to bind Satan and loose the Spirit of God. The problem is that Satan pretends that he didn't get the message. Instead, he proceeds with guerrilla warfare against the saints of God. Satan has no *legal* right to attack us, but he can still render us useless if we allow him to. Jesus said that the gates of hell will not prevail against His church. Instead of Satan taking over our territory, we are to take over his.

Where do we get the strength and authority to order the devil around? Luke 10:1-20 records the story of how Jesus sent seventy disciples out in pairs to preach in the surrounding villages. He also gave them authority over *"all the power of the enemy"* (Luke 10:19). This meant that the demons were subject to them. The disciples were able to cast out demons because they carried the authority of Christ, who has power over every demon.

Jesus has given us the same authority. As believers, we have a God-given assignment on this earth to bind the forces of evil and loose the love and saving power of God. As part of the Lord's body, we have both the authority and the power to tread on the enemy.

We Have the Weapons

People without Christ are under the bondage and control of Satan and usually resist our efforts to bring them to the Lord. We cannot change another person's will in such a matter by scheming or plotting or by trying to manipulate him or her. This is a spiritual battle that we can neither wage nor win with physical resources. Our commanding General, however, has provided us with very effective spiritual weapons:

> *For though we walk in the flesh, we do not war according to the flesh, for the weapons of our warfare are not of the flesh, but divinely powerful for the destruction of fortresses. We are destroying speculations and every lofty thing raised up against the knowledge of God, and we are taking every thought captive to the obedience of Christ* (2 Corinthians 10:3–5).

Many times, we mistakenly fight with human, emotional, and psychological weapons. We argue, try to convince, and maybe even coerce people into listening to our message. When none of this works, we assume that God has refused our prayers. That is not the case. Our problem was in using the wrong weapons. What we should have done was bind the enemy, intercede in faith, ask God to prepare the soil of their hearts to receive the good seed, and then plant the Word. In His own time and way, the Lord will the cause seed to sprout and grow.

I remember a woman who was saved shortly after her husband died, while their children were in their twenties. The children were taking drugs and she was tormented with fear because they were all unsaved. It was a great trial for her, especially being alone after the death of her husband.

One night as the woman was praying for her children, as she had done time and time again, God spoke to her and said, "Leave your children with Me. It is My will to save them, so stop distressing yourself." From that night on, the mother never again worried about the salvation of her children. She stopped cooking up schemes to get them saved. Instead, she said, "They are God's problem," and continued to pray.

One morning at four o'clock, she was startled from sleep by a telephone call from her son, who said, "I have heard the voice of God. What should I do?" Right there on the phone, she led him to the Lord.

Soon, that young man became Spirit-filled, attended Bible college, and became an assistant pastor in Tulsa, Oklahoma. Today, every member of this woman's family is saved because she allowed God to work in their lives rather than try to save them herself.

If you are praying for someone and the circumstances still look bad after you pray, hang in there; God will work things out eventually. This mother was patient and waited faithfully on the Lord. She believed God's promise and received what she desired.

Whale Songs

Sometimes, when you pray and trust God to change the will of a rebellious loved one, but nothing happens, your faith can really be put to the test. Once doubts start creeping in, you may be tempted to take matters into your own hands. If you are impatient over your unanswered petitions and are ready to give up, remember some of the marvelous biblical examples of how God works on the wills of rebels.

God commanded the prophet Jonah to travel to the city of Nineveh and preach repentance. Since the people of Nineveh were traditional enemies of Israel, Jonah did not want to go. Instead, he was determined to run from God. His will was set. God, however, was just as determined to give the city of Nineveh a chance to repent.

One of God's ways to deal with His servants is to make it difficult to disobey. Jonah boarded a ship for Tarshish—which was in the opposite direction from Nineveh. God caused a great storm to blow up, which threatened to sink the ship along with Jonah and its crew. When the crew learned that Jonah was running from God, they threw him overboard. Immediately the storm stopped, and God sent a great whale (or fish) to swallow Jonah.

During three days in the belly of the whale, Jonah had plenty of time to reflect on his rebellion and developed a whole new attitude. He repented of his disobedience, and God set him free from the fish. Jonah promptly traveled to Nineveh as he was told, preached in the city, and witnessed the outbreak of a great revival! If Jonah had never gone, thousands of rebels would have been lost.

God has plenty more whales where Jonah's came from, enough for all the rebels that you know. If you don't do what God tells you to do, who could be lost? How many families would never know Jesus? How many people might never be healed because you gave up too soon?

Recently, Wally and I were at a special dinner where most of the guests were unsaved. The dinner was in honor of a young couple, and the young man had just received Christ as his Savior. He was on fire for the Lord! Seated next to him was his unsaved brother, who offered him a cigarette.

"No, thanks," he said, "I don't smoke."

The brother was surprised because this young man had always smoked. "Why did you just suddenly stop?" he asked.

This wonderful young man replied, "I had orders from above."

Later during this same dinner, the young man's father listened to the Gospel with an open heart and was almost ready to receive Christ. This young man, newly born again, is bringing light to his entire household, and I believe that someday that entire family will come to Jesus.

Never underestimate what God can do with a rebellious heart!

Rebel With a Dark Cause

Saul of Tarsus was another rebel, one who actually killed Christians just because they were Christians. A devout Pharisee, Saul thought he was doing his duty to God by persecuting Christians. Although he was sincere, he was sincerely wrong. In the name of God, Saul was doing the devil's work, because the devil is a murderer.

There must have been some people who brought the power of prayer against the forces of darkness that controlled Saul's will. One of those who prayed may even have been Stephen, who was stoned to death for his faith while Saul stood by as a witness. Stephen's dying words were a prayer: *"Lord, do not hold this sin against them!"* (Acts 7:60)

"Never underestimate what God can do with a rebellious heart!"

Saul was on his way to Damascus to arrest and persecute more Christians when he was struck down by a bright light and heard the voice of the Lord speaking to him. After three days of blindness with time to think things over, Saul became a devoted follower of Jesus Christ. With a new will and a new name, Paul became the greatest evangelist of the early church and the author of thirteen books of the New Testament.

What happened to change Paul so radically? This rebel got his heart and mind in tune with wisdom from above, and he got his will in line with God's will. Through Paul, former rebel and now willing servant, God changed the world.

All Things Are Possible With God

Years ago, people would say to me, "If you are praying for someone to be saved, you have to keep in mind that every person has a will, and you cannot overcome someone's will." I got into a pattern of looking at God's Word and then looking at the person's will and becoming discouraged because I could see that he or she really did not want to serve the Lord. I was putting human will above the power of God.

Before Wally and I were married, I asked him if he felt called into the ministry, since I did not want to marry a minister. He assured me that he did not feel called at all. I said, "I do not ever want to be in the ministry."

"Don't worry," he answered, "it won't happen."

About three years after we got married, Wally began to come home every weekend saying, "Oh, I feel called into the ministry." God was in the process of changing Wally's will.

You may be saying, "I will never serve God full-time." Perhaps not, but don't count on it. If God has called you, He knows how to get through to you. Today, I am in the ministry, and I have never been happier in my life. At one time I was as rebellious as anyone else, but people were praying for me and standing on the Word for me. Gradually, my thoughts and will became more and more conformed to those of the Lord until today I want nothing more than to obey Him and serve Him faithfully.

If you are discouraged and doubtful about whether or not someone you are praying for will ever change, just remember: God changed you, didn't He? All of us were once rebels against the Lord, yet He drew us with His love, brought us to the cross, and made us new creatures in Him. Think back to the time before you were born again. Weren't you a rebel making decisions with the wisdom of the world? Someone interceded for you—someone you may not even know personally—and your will was changed. If God could change me and if He could change you, is there anyone He *cannot* change? Jesus said, *"All things are possible to him who believes"* (Mark 9:23).

Don't give up on your intercession. Keep on bringing that person before the Lord. Trust that in time, God will change the heart of that person to be responsive to the Gospel. Also, watch out for the "Word thief." As you intercede for the unsaved, the father of lies will get more and more irritated and agitated. He does not want those souls saved and will do everything he can to distract you. He will whisper lies in your ear to discourage your faith and to sow doubt. He will try to get you so caught up in worldly cares and worldly wisdom that you will stop interceding and cause your "harvest" to rot in the fields.

The Heart of a King

God can change the wills of people who are not Christians as well as those of Christians who are living in rebellion. Our part in this process is to be faithful in intercession. Our prayers can result in God's moving the hearts even of people we do not know and will never meet in this life. This includes leaders of nations and other prominent persons on the global scene. The Bible says that the hearts of kings are in the hands of God: *"The king's heart is like channels of water in the hand of the Lord; He turns it wherever He wishes"* (Proverbs 21:1).

Here are just a few of the biblical kings whose hearts God turned to His will, even if they did not recognize it: Ahasuerus (see Esther 6, Nehemiah 2); Nebuchadnezzar (see Ezekiel 29:18, Daniel 4); Cyrus (see Ezra 1:1, Isaiah 44:28); Darius (see Ezra 6:22); and Augustus (see Luke 2:1–7).

If God changed the hearts of ancient kings, He can change the hearts of twenty-first-century leaders. Our part as intercessors is to come against evil spirits that are over nations and over leaders of nations. As we besiege those strongholds, God can take the hearts of the leaders and turn them the way they should go to bless their nations.

In the time of Ezra, the Israelites were returning to Israel after seventy years of exile. They longed to rebuild their city and their temple, but they had no money. Standing in faith, they took the matter to God in prayer. God touched the heart of Cyrus, the Persian king, who issued a decree allowing all the Jews to go home. He also provided money for rebuilding the temple.

Such developments can happen only when believers behind the scenes pray and bind the rulers of darkness. Through Christ, we have great power and authority, even over the destiny of entire nations. Our problem is that we so seldom exercise them.

Two Information Networks

All of us listen to one or the other of two sources of wisdom and information: either God or the devil. The third chapter of James tells us about these two kinds of wisdom. First, there is the "wisdom" of this world:

> *But if you have bitter jealousy and selfish ambition in your heart, do not be arrogant and so lie against the truth. This wisdom is not that which comes down from above, but is earthly, natural, demonic. For where jealousy and selfish ambition exist, there is disorder and every evil thing* (James 3:14–16).

This kind of "wisdom" produces fear and leads eventually to death. The second kind of wisdom—God's wisdom—is the exact opposite:

> *But the wisdom from above is first pure, then peaceable, gentle, reasonable, full of mercy and good fruits, unwavering, without hypocrisy.*

> *And the seed whose fruit is righteousness is sown in peace by those who make peace* (James 3:17–18).

This kind of wisdom produces faith and leads to life.

Our job is to decide which kind of wisdom is going to inform and motivate our wills. God wants to draw all men to Himself; He wants everyone to come to repentance. There is a hindering force, however—a spirit that will snatch God's Word from people's hearts and bring confusion and blindness to their minds. Paul said:

"Which wisdom will inform and motivate your will?"

> *And even if our gospel is veiled, it is veiled to those who are perishing, in whose case the god of this world has blinded the minds of the unbelieving so that they might not see the light of the gospel of the glory of Christ, who is the image of God* (2 Corinthians 4:3–4).

Men and women who are not walking with Jesus draw from worldly wisdom. They have no knowledge of the heavenly wisdom that is pure and gentle. Every decision they make comes from the earthly wisdom that controls their mind and their will.

In chapter 7 of Romans, Paul described his own struggle between his old nature of sin, which was so prone to evil, and his new nature in Christ, which sought to serve God. He was in a constant war of wills, doing things which he did not want to do and not doing what he wanted to do. It was a war of the flesh versus the spirit.

There are many people who are in this state. In their innermost being they want to serve the Lord, but they are bound by earthly wisdom or a weak will. Like Paul, however, we can thank God for His provision in Christ! Jesus Christ has set us free from the authority of sin in our lives and from the evil influences both within and without that once governed our wills. We need to declare our freedom and continually pray that other people will see their opportunity and choose to be free.

Forget "Plan B"

Have you ever prayed with what you call faith, while all the time making alternate plans just in case God does not "come through"? That is what the Bible calls being *"double-minded."* If you do not know God's will on a matter, you should pray for wisdom, guidance, and clear counsel. Once you know God's revealed will, you can pray without hesitation, without doubt, and in complete faith, knowing that you will receive your petition. Jesus said, *"Ask, and it will be given to you."*

Faith is agreeing with God's Word concerning a need and then acting like it will actually happen. God said He would answer the prayer of faith. Is your prayer of faith conditional? The Word of God says that if you believe, you will receive.

Our prayers and intercession are important because they have an effect on what happens in the world. Jesus said that we are salt and light on the earth:

> *You are the salt of the earth; but if the salt has become tasteless, how can it be made salty again? It is no longer good for anything, except to be thrown out and trampled under foot by men. You are the light of the world. A city set on a hill cannot be hidden; nor does anyone light a lamp and put it under a basket, but on the lampstand, and it gives light to all who are in the house. Let your light shine before men in such a way that they may see your good works, and glorify your Father who is in heaven* (Matthew 5:13–16).

Salt is a preservative and overcomes the tendency to disintegrate and decay. As the salt of the earth, we are to overcome the decay of the world. The world would already have destroyed itself because of its filth and rottenness if it were not for the salt of the earth. Because of the nature of God in us, we are hindering that destruction.

Light causes the darkness to flee. The darkness does not have a choice. Since God is our source of light, we will continue to shine regardless of the way those who *"sit in darkness"* respond. Our light source is inextinguishable! It is our faith that overcomes the world, regardless of what the world wills or thinks! We don't need an alternate plan. God's original "Plan A" is perfect!

Resting in God

Do you think God is too slow in answering your prayers for another's salvation? When we care for someone we are tempted to get impatient and take things into our own hands. Let the "Lord of the harvest" decide when harvest time is to come. If you set a certain date for someone to get saved and turn his or her life over to God, you may want to give up if it doesn't happen according to your deadline. God does not want you to give up; therefore, do not set a time for your harvest and don't quit praying! Keep planting the seed, using your weapons, and interceding until God's time comes, and your "rebel" is in the body of Christ.

Don't try to "help" God with His master plan. Stop trying to use natural methods to fight a spiritual battle—it won't work! We are human, but we can't fight a spiritual war with human methods. Instead, we must use God's mighty weapons to knock down the devil's strongholds. With these weapons we can conquer their rebellious ideas and teach them to obey Christ. We cannot change other people's wills through our own actions. Our job is to bring the unsaved and the rebellious before God in prayer.

It is not your effort that brings about answers to your prayers. You cannot use your will to overcome the will of another. Do not allow yourself to become weary and tired from continuing on in your own strength. Only the power of God can break down the strongholds. Using His power does not require yours. Simply trust that your God and His Word will do the work. Let the Lord deal with the other person's free will. Faithfully perform the task God gave to you and trust Him to honor His Word. He knows how to handle people.

Remember that your faith is in God and in His Word. When you have been faithful in intercession for another, then rest. Trust God to do His work. If, on occasion, a person's will has not changed, leave that to God also. He loves that person more than you do and knows exactly how to deal with him or her. If you have unanswered questions in a situation, remember Deuteronomy 29:29: "*The secret things belong to the* L*ORD our God, but the things revealed belong to us and to our sons forever, that we may observe all the words of this law.*" Your task is to act on the "revealed things" and trust God with those things that you don't understand.

In the end, remember that faith is not complicated; we have made it so. God-pleasing faith is *simple* faith without all the "extras" we are so prone to add. We must come to the Lord with faith like little children—simple, trusting, persevering, and confident. Childlike faith will change your life, make you prosperous, and bring you health and victory. It also will be powerful in helping to change the minds and hearts of people you care about so that they will come to know the Lord as well.

If you want a faith that *works*, then come to the Lord like a child. Childlike faith *always* pleases God—and opens the windows of heaven!

STEPS TO A SIMPLER FAITH

1. List some signs that might reveal one's rebellion against God's will. Ask God to show you if you have any of these characteristics in your life.
2. Find five examples from the Bible of rebellious wills being changed. Note the verses in your Scripture notebook.
3. Meditate on James 3:13–18 from your Bible. Write out the two kinds of wisdom and knowledge from which men can receive wisdom. Choose one nation whose ruler is not acting in the wisdom of God. Resolve to intercede for this ruler and nation.
4. Study this last chapter and find some faith confessions you can use to pray for unsaved relatives and friends.
5. Starting today, be especially alert to messages of "worldly wisdom" (in the media, at the office, in conversations with friends). Ask God to bring His light of truth to the dark world of counterfeit wisdom.

Endnotes

1. Clifton Fadiman and André Bernard, eds., *Bartlett's Book of Anecdotes, Revised Edition* (New York: Little, Brown and Company, 2000), 41.
2. *Merriam Webster's Collegiate Dictionary*, 10th ed. (Springfield, Massachusetts: Merriam-Webster, Inc., 1996).
3. W. E. Vine, Merrill F. Unger, William White, Jr., *Vine's Complete Expository Dictionary of Old and New Testament Words* (Nashville: Thomas Nelson Publishers, 1996), New Testament section, 683.
4. Vine, *Vine's Expository Dictionary*, 683.
5. Vine, *Vine's Expository Dictionary*, 400.
6. *Nelson's Illustrated Bible Dictionary* (Nashville: Thomas Nelson Publishers, 1968).
7. Kenneth Copeland, *Prayer: Your Foundation for Success* (Fort Worth, Texas: KCP Publications, 1983), pp. 13-14.
8. Don Gossett, *What You Say Is What You Get!* (Springdale, Pennsylvania: Whitaker House, 1976).
9. Jerry Savelle, *Prosperity of the Soul*.